EQUITY VALUATION

Science, Art, or Craft?

Frank J. Fabozzi, CFA, Sergio M. Focardi, and Caroline Jonas

CFA Institute
Research
Foundation

Statement of Purpose

The CFA Institute Research Foundation is a not-for-profit organization established to promote the development and dissemination of relevant research for investment practitioners worldwide.

SUSTAINABLE FORESTRY INITIATIVE

Certified Sourcing

www.sfiprogram.org

SFI-01681

Biographies

Frank J. Fabozzi, CFA, is professor of finance at EDHEC Business School and a senior scientific adviser at EDHEC-Risk Institute (Nice, France). He is editor of the *Journal of Portfolio Management* and a trustee for the BlackRock closed-end fund complex. The author of numerous books on asset management and four CFA Institute Research Foundation monographs, Professor Fabozzi is the 2007 recipient of the C. Stewart Sheppard Award and the 2015 recipient of the James R. Vertin Award, both from CFA Institute. He was also the 2002 inductee to the Fixed Income Analysts Society Hall of Fame. Professor Fabozzi received his bachelor's degree in economics and statistics and his master's degree in economics from the City College of New York and his PhD in economics from the City University of New York.

Sergio M. Focardi is professor of finance at Leonard de Vinci University (Paris-La Défense, France) and a founding partner of The Intertek Group. He serves on the editorial board of the *Journal of Portfolio Management* and has co-authored numerous articles and books, including the CFA Institute Research Foundation monographs *Investment Management: A Science to Teach or an Art to Learn?*, *Investment Management after the Global Financial Crisis*, and *Challenges in Quantitative Equity Management*, and the award-winning books *Financial Modeling of the Equity Market: From CAPM to Cointegration* and *The Mathematics of Financial Modeling and Investment Management*. Professor Focardi also co-authored *Financial Econometrics: From Basics to Advanced Modeling Techniques* and *Robust Portfolio Optimization and Management*. He received his degree in electronic engineering from the University of Genoa and his PhD in finance from the University of Karlsruhe.

Caroline Jonas is a managing partner of The Intertek Group in Paris, where she is responsible for research projects. Jonas is co-author of numerous reports and books on finance and technology and of three CFA Institute Research Foundation monographs, including *Investment Management: A Science to Teach or an Art to Learn?* and *Investment Management after the Global Financial Crisis*. She received her bachelor's degree from the University of Illinois at Urbana-Champaign.

Contents

CE Qualified Activity CFA Institute This publication qualifies for 2 CE credits under the guidelines of the CFA Institute Continuing Education Program.

Acknowledgments

The authors wish to thank those from academia and the industry who accepted the challenge to articulate their views on equity valuation. Their perspectives are cited and attributed throughout this monograph.

We are also grateful to the CFA Institute Research Foundation for funding this project and, in particular, to its director of research, Laurence B. Siegel, and its executive director, Walter (Bud) Haslett, CFA, for their encouragement, assistance, and insightful comments.

Foreword

Where do stock prices come from? The easy answer is that they are the outcome of supply and demand; that is, the price of any given stock is that which causes the quantity supplied to equal the quantity demanded.

Of course, that answer, like most easy answers, is unsatisfying. What causes the supply and demand for a stock to be what it is? There are two sets of players in the game that we call the stock market: (1) the *sell side*, consisting of issuers (seekers of capital) and their agents, called "investment bankers" or "stockbrokers,"[1] and (2) the *buy side*, consisting of saver-investors (providers of capital) and *their* agents, called "investment managers."

Each of these characters in the financial zoo presumably has a view on every asset in the world, the view generally being that one should ignore the asset. There are simply too many assets for everyone to analyze, so they delegate the task of analyzing most assets to other investors, who—through their collective wisdom, it is believed—will agree on a price that makes the asset a fair deal; in that case, the asset is held in an index fund. (In an environment where index funds exist, simply *not holding* an asset expresses a strong negative view on that asset and is in no way equivalent to holding the asset at its index weight.)

It is only when an investor believes an asset offers a *better-than-fair* deal—either because it is cheap, justifying an above-index weight, or because it is expensive, requiring a below-index weight—that he or she becomes an active manager with respect to that asset.

Active managers contribute to the price discovery process by shifting the demand curve for that asset—outward, if they are buyers—in a way that an index fund investor does not do. Active managers also affect the supply curve by offering stocks for sale. Finally, sell-siders (corporations and their investment banker agents) may also be regarded as active managers in that they, too, hold nonindex weights of the assets they trade and thus move the supply and demand curves for stocks in exactly the same way that buy-siders do.

Well, in almost the same way. A corporation has only one stock to sell; an investment manager can choose from among all the stocks offered for sale in the world. Thus, the corporate issuer's impact is more concentrated, and the investment manager's impact is more diffuse. But the underlying Economics 101 of asset price discovery is the same when viewed from either side.

---

[1]They are also called "broker/dealers"—the word "dealer" highlighting the market-making or principal function of the institution, in contrast to the buyer–seller matching or agent function.

In a 2003 article,[2] Barton Waring and I described active managers as *forecasters*—people who

> use the information available to them, and whatever their native talents are, to make stock-by-stock (or factor-by-factor, or market-by-market) forecasts of pure active return based on information that they believe is not yet impounded in the price, and then they translate these forecasts into portfolios.

Through this activity they add alpha—or hope to. With the benefit of 15 years of additional reflection, however, I'd like to rephrase Barton's and my description of asset managers as forecasters to say that they are *disagree-ers* (if that is a word). By making forecasts "based on information that they believe is not ... impounded in the price," active managers are people whose forecasts are different enough from the consensus to justify, at least in their own minds, betting other people's money and their own reputations on the validity of their disagreement.

It bears repeating that a majority of these disagreements with the consensus are *not* justified: Most active managers are beaten by their benchmarks over most periods and eventually eat humble pie. Yet there are active managers—enough to be much more than a statistical accident—who do beat the "market" (that is, their fairly chosen benchmark). Inquiring how these successful managers make their correct nonconsensus forecasts is a worthwhile pursuit.

Frank Fabozzi, Sergio Focardi, and Caroline Jonas have, in a series of remarkable and well-received CFA Institute Research Foundation monographs, developed a survey-based strategy for investigating important issues in investment finance. In the past, they have turned their attention to (1) quantitative finance, (2) quantitative equity investing, (3) the investment management industry after the global financial crisis, and (4) the distinction between art and science in the investment management profession.[3]

---

[2]M. Barton Waring and Laurence B. Siegel, "The Dimensions of Active Management," *Journal of Portfolio Management* (Spring 2003): 35–51.

[3]Frank J. Fabozzi, Sergio M. Focardi, and Caroline Jonas, *Trends in Quantitative Finance* (Charlottesville, VA: CFA Institute Research Foundation, 2006); Frank J. Fabozzi, Sergio M. Focardi, and Caroline Jonas, *Challenges in Quantitative Equity Management* (Charlottesville, VA: CFA Institute Research Foundation, 2008); Frank J. Fabozzi, Sergio M. Focardi, and Caroline Jonas, *Investment Management after the Global Financial Crisis* (Charlottesville, VA: CFA Institute Research Foundation, 2010); Frank J. Fabozzi, Sergio M. Focardi, and Caroline Jonas, *Investment Management: A Science to Teach or an Art to Learn?* (Charlottesville, VA: CFA Institute Research Foundation, 2014).

In this, their fifth research monograph, the authors investigate how analysts employed by active investment managers form their nonconsensus beliefs—their conviction that a stock offers a better-than-fair deal either to those who buy it (or overweight it) because it is cheap or to those who sell it (or underweight it) because it is expensive. They interview analysts, portfolio managers, directors of research, and chief investment officers at a variety of firms in countries in both Europe and North America.

The authors' insights into the "science, art, or craft" of equity analysis reflect and amplify the diligent work of the many investment professionals who agreed to open up their work lives in these interviews. We are delighted to present this excellent monograph, and we hope to hear from these authors many more times in the future.

Laurence B. Siegel
Gary P. Brinson Director of Research
CFA Institute Research Foundation
November 2017

Preface

Fundamental analysts and fundamental active managers believe that one can determine the intrinsic (fundamental) value of a company's stock by analyzing the company. They argue that their ability to estimate the difference between a stock's fundamental price and its market price allows them to outperform the market, thereby keeping markets at least somewhat efficient while creating value (alpha) for their clients. Much of the academic community agrees and has developed valuation models, such as present value models based on fundamental analysis. Such models include the widely used dividend discount model, market-multiplier models (such as the popular price-to-earnings models), and asset- and options-based valuation models.

Studies show, however, that on average and over time, despite all the fundamental research, active traditional managers fail to outperform markets. This fact, plus a number of other aspects, including widely published studies showing that, on average, high-fee funds do not perform as well as less expensive funds,[4] has resulted in what the data provider Morningstar (Morningstar Manager Research 2017) calls "a sea-change in investor preferences" (p. 1). The Morningstar Manager Research report on annual US asset flows shows that for the full year 2016, investors withdrew almost $264 billion from actively managed US equity funds. And the withdrawals occurred despite a trend toward stocks versus bonds as the S&P 500 Index closed up 12% for the year. For the same period, passively managed US equity funds saw net inflows of almost $237 billion. In their *Wall Street Journal* article, Tergesen and Zweig (2016) cite Morningstar estimates that passive assets under management since 2007 have tripled to $5.7 trillion, whereas assets in active funds have increased by only 54%, to $23.2 trillion.

Still, according to Morningstar, 66% of US mutual fund and exchange-traded fund assets are actively invested, albeit down from 84% just 10 years ago.

But these percentages could change soon. Representing less than 20% of US equity holdings by retail (individual) investors only a decade ago, passive funds' share of US equities is expected to reach 50% in 2018–2019 (Morningstar Manager Research 2017).

While the trend to passive equity funds is particularly pronounced in the United States, it is also present in Europe, where passive equity funds now

---

[4]According to Morningstar, the average asset-weighted annual fee for actively managed US stock funds is currently 0.78%, compared with 0.11% for the average passive stock fund.

attract more net flows than active equity funds, and in the Asia-Pacific region, where net flows to passive strategies now almost match flows to active strategies.

This monograph addresses a number of questions these trends raise:

- Public stocks are traded in competitive markets and subject to the law of supply and demand: Is there really such a thing as an intrinsic (or fundamental) value of a stock? If yes, can we determine this value using the tools we presently have? Or can we determine only relative values?

- What about determining the value of hard-to-value assets, such as initial public offerings or private equity? What is the role of "hype" (hyperbole) or information asymmetry in determining value?

- Assuming that fundamental active analysts/managers can estimate the intrinsic value of a stock and spot mispricings by comparing the intrinsic price to the market price, can they execute an advantageous trade that delivers value to the investor? What tools and heuristics do such analysts use, and how effective are they?

- Do economic or other phenomena, such as quantitative easing by central banks or corporate stock buybacks, distort market prices, taking them far from a stock's fundamental price?

- What is the equilibrium between the cost and the benefit of doing fundamental analysis, where the benefit is alpha or extra return to the investor?

- Do fundamental analysts/managers really play an important role in keeping markets (quasi) efficient?

- Will news sources, data sources, new tools, or new technology not yet (widely) used allow fundamental managers to better estimate a stock's fundamental value?

- Has the global investment universe changed so much that the role of the fundamental analyst/manager is no longer central? In other words, are there better ways to generate returns for investors than traditional value investing?

Quotations in this book that are not attributed to a source listed in the References are from academic and industry colleagues who provided us with their views on equity valuation in a series of interviews during the first half of 2017.

1. Finance Theory and Equity Valuation

"Any valuation must be in accord with the well-established theory of finance." That is the first of three conditions Stephen Penman (2016, p. 3), professor of accounting at Columbia Business School, identifies for obtaining more robust equity valuations than we currently can obtain—something that must be of interest to the industry. So, let's start here and see whether commonly used valuation practices are indeed in accord with finance theory.

The conceptual foundation of fundamental analysis is a supporting pillar of the notion of the true or intrinsic price of stocks, and the question of equity valuation is closely related to the question of market efficiency. Thus, a proper analysis of valuation issues cannot be made without a minimum of theory and macroeconomic considerations.

Sébastien Lleo, who, before joining NEOMA Business School (France) as a finance professor, had nine years of experience in financial markets, remarked,

> The concept of fundamental (or intrinsic) value rationalizes and frames our search for the "true" value of an asset. It is the value against which we assess today's price to determine whether an investment is overvalued, undervalued, or fairly valued. This makes it one of the most important constructs in investment theory, and one of the most important ideas in investment practice.

Let's start by observing that in any attempt to evaluate the "true" value of a firm's stock, fundamental analysis seems to be an obvious and natural approach: An investor considering an investment in equities will probably start by looking at a number of firms in an attempt to estimate the stream of future revenues that each firm might provide. In so doing, the investor will likely follow the advice of two Columbia Business School professors, Benjamin Graham and David Dodd, who wrote the textbook *Security Analysis: Principles and Techniques* (1934). Initially intended as a common-sense guide to investing, the book, first published in 1934, had by the time of Graham's death in 1988 become the reference text for almost all subsequent work in fundamental analysis.

As Graham and Dodd advocate, the investor, after analyzing a firm as a potential investment, will look at the market price to determine whether the firm's revenue streams are in line with its market price—that is, whether a stock's actual market price is in line with its "true" value.

Because of the difficulty in determining a stock's true value, Graham recommends that investors invest with a *margin of safety*; that is, investors should put money into stocks priced at a discount sufficiently large, when compared with a reasonable estimate of what the stock is worth, to make the investment attractive even if the estimate is a little too high. Not only single stocks but whole sectors of the markets might be trading at a discount. For example, a 2016 study by BlackRock found that over the past decade, global value stocks, including energy and materials, were trading at a 20% discount relative to the broader market.

At the time of Graham and Dodd's original work, fundamental analysis was not yet highly formalized. It was based on educated economic common sense. Investing would become increasingly more complicated with the introduction of the notion of *risk*. With that notion added, the price at which a stock is traded in the market reflects not only the company's ability to generate cash but also the risk associated with future streams of cash flows. And ultimately, the price of each asset will be set by the supply of and demand for that asset.

As discussed in textbooks on the classical theory of asset pricing, financial asset prices are equal to the sum of the discounted values of expected future cash flows. The discount rate is determined as the sum of the risk-free rates and a risk premium; it is exogenous and cannot be determined by purely financial considerations.

In classical finance, however, a parallel framework relates to the notion of market efficiency and intrinsic prices. This framework has become important for both theoretical and practical reasons. A first definition of market efficiency comes from Eugene F. Fama (1970), who stated that unfettered financial markets are efficient. Campbell Harvey, a professor of finance at Duke University's Fuqua School of Business, commented,

> This [efficiency], according to Fama, means that market prices correctly reflect all relevant information. This statement of market inefficiency is often misunderstood. In Fama's most extreme scenario, efficiency [exists when] prices correctly reflect all public and private information at any point in time. In a second scenario, prices are assumed to reflect all publicly available information. This means that any trading strategy based on publicly available information should not earn excess returns. However, neither of these scenarios is particularly realistic. It is naive to think that prices correctly reflect all public or public and private information. Indeed, the statements are not even testable given that we never observe "true" prices. So, a reasonable starting point is the concept of *relative efficiency*. It is more likely that prices of large-cap US equities correctly reflect information than that

they do so on the Zimbabwe stock exchange. There is likely some degree of mispricing in the US, but the degree of mispricing is likely a lot larger in Zimbabwe.

Harvey continued,

If we view the price of financial assets—in our case, equities—as equal to the sum of expected values of discounted future cash flows, the entire question of market efficiency and the existence of an intrinsic price hinges on the ability to get as close as possible to the "true" discount rates and expected cash flows. We will never get it exactly right—nor will we know how close we are—however, if we are closer [at estimating] the intrinsic price than others are, there is a possibility of making excess returns.

The job of the financial analyst, then, is to discover whether a financial asset is mispriced (that is, under- or overpriced with respect to its intrinsic value or a comparable asset) under the assumption that markets will eventually correct the mispricing. The identification of and the ability to take advantage of mispricings (or price anomalies) are believed to generate profit when asset prices revert to their true price (or when correct relative prices are reinstated).

Although markets are driven by supply and demand, it is widely believed that intrinsic value still plays a role in delivering better returns. Kenneth Little, managing director of the investments group at the value investment firm Brandes Investment Partners, remarked,

Fundamental (intrinsic) value can still be used as an effective tool to outperform the market, but only for investors that have a sufficiently long time horizon. While it is difficult to define how long this time horizon needs to be, we assume that in any period of less than five years, the stock price returns may be driven at least as much by factors such as momentum, flow of funds, and investor sentiment.

Matteo Bonaventura, a buy-side analyst at the Milan-based asset manager Banor SIM, commented,

I think that intrinsic value does exist, but its estimation requires research, and it therefore represents a (huge) cost. Thus, in order for this process to turn profitable, market prices have to be far from intrinsic values, and this is most likely when large information asymmetries exist. For example, take the Italian stock exchange, Borsa Italiana, in the period 2012–2017. Some less researched companies delivered an astonishing 500% total return in this period, which means roughly a 40% annual return, compared to 10.4% for the overall market for the same period. Analysts and portfolio managers who were able to better understand the fundamentals underlying these companies undoubtedly benefited.

However, I think that intrinsic values are dynamic and can change with major nonanticipated shocks in supply and demand. For example, the recent tax advantage on long-term investments in Italian small caps drove the stock prices up to very high valuation multiples. Thus, in my opinion, both considerations have to be taken into account when thinking about intrinsic value.

The €205 billion Dutch fund PGGM Investments is a long-term investor and uses the notion of intrinsic value to construct fundamental portfolios. Jaap van Dam, the firm's principal director of investment strategy, commented,

> Intrinsic value can be used in a very narrow sense, to measure book value. But you can broaden this a bit in the sense that intrinsic value can be used, for example, if you invest deeply in understanding how firms create long-term value. This requires an understanding of the firm, its markets, strategies, investor stewardship; in the long term, there are a lot of agency issues. The market price is a question of supply and demand, but behind the market price, one can reasonably estimate a ballpark number that represents the firm's value. We use intrinsic price not to "beat the market"—a term I don't like—but to generate better returns.

Christian Kjaer, head of global equities and volatility at the $113 billion Danish state pension fund ATP, remarked,

> In the space of global equities, we consider the uncertainties around various valuation models to be huge. Consequently, we need to observe rather extreme mispricing relative to the fundamental model value in order to have sufficient conviction in the perceived mispricing. In areas where we consider our fundamental understanding to be stronger—for example, Danish equities—we have significantly more confidence in perceived fundamental mispricings and use it [this information] more actively to outperform markets.

The role of theory is to provide rules that allow a financial analyst to make forecasts. Consider sending a satellite into orbit. Doing so would be impossible without the theory of gravity. Theory allows a physicist to use data to determine the satellite's future path. In finance, however, we are in an intermediate situation; that is, to determine the future path of an asset's price, we need knowledge of some basic facts, plus the ability to test whether those facts are true. Unlike in physics, in finance (and economics), we do not have the ability to test our theories. In equity valuation, we can avoid abstract mathematical and statistical principles, but we need an understanding of the theoretical underpinnings of valuation.

In free markets, the price of "things" is determined by the interaction between supply and demand—with links, possibly complex ones, between the characteristics of "things" and their prices. Largely dependent on objective characteristics, competition assigns a market price to goods and services in common use. The price of a car, for example, depends on the vehicle's size, power, speed, and other features. But this dependence of price on characteristics is not linear and can become highly nonlinear for vehicles that reach the limits of performance and/or benefit from strong marketing/advertising campaigns.

This nonlinearity in pricing is typical of things whose price is subject to nonobjective characteristics, such as fads or branding, where social or other motivations, such as "herding to have," contribute to determining the price. In economics, these goods are often referred to as "Veblen goods," from the Norwegian-American economist Thorstein Veblen, who analyzed the motivation for consumption in the US economy at the end of the nineteenth century. Veblen introduced the notion of "conspicuous consumption" to identify the type of consumption that is not related to the direct fruition of the goods consumed but to the goods' symbolic value. But even in this case, the law of supply and demand holds, as it holds in art markets, where the intrinsic value of a work of art is ill defined and its market price is the amount of money someone is willing to pay at any given time. Alternative proposals for pricing, such as determining the value of things with respect to the skill or time needed to produce them, as proposed by Karl Marx, among others, run contrary to the spirit of free markets.

Free competitive markets for goods and services should be reasonably free from arbitrage opportunities. So the "law of one price" should hold, approximately. Exceptions are frequent, however. For example, with the introduction of revenue maximization strategies, the price of an airline seat or hotel room changes rapidly as a function of supply and demand, and different agents may offer the same seat or hotel room at a different price. Violations of the law of one price do not disrupt the market for goods and services because physical impediments prevent fully exploiting arbitrage. To summarize, in free competitive markets, goods and services do not have an intrinsic price but respect (approximately) the law of one price.

What about financial markets? Financial assets trade in markets that are almost perfectly competitive and free. Neoclassical finance theory assumes that the prices of financial assets are free from true arbitrage opportunities, though financial markets might exhibit "near arbitrage"—that is, the possibility of small gains with limited risk. And these gains (and the risk) can become large if pursued with the use of leverage. A number of papers, including one by Shleifer and Vishny (1997), have found that financial markets present near-arbitrage opportunities but that exploiting these opportunities can be difficult because of the decision-making process of economic agents.

In the absence of arbitrage, the price of a financial asset is the sum of the expected cash flows discounted with market discount rates, where the discount rate includes a risk premium. This principle applies to all competitive financial markets devoid of arbitrage opportunities. In itself, the principle characterizes neither intrinsic price nor market efficiency.

The notion of intrinsic price requires the introduction of macroeconomic considerations. Intrinsic price is a concept related to equilibrium in a specific macroeconomic theory. Both the notion of intrinsic price and that of deviations from the intrinsic price can be defined only within a supply-and-demand framework. Simply stated, the intrinsic price is the price financial assets would have in economies where the supply and demand for investments are in equilibrium.

As Cochrane (2001) states in the preface to his book *Asset Pricing*,

> Asset pricing theory shares the positive versus normative tension present in the rest of economics. Does it describe the way the world does work, or the way the world should work? We observe the prices or returns of many assets. We can use the theory positively, to try to understand why prices or returns are what they are. If the world does not obey a model's predictions, we can decide that the model needs improvement. However, we can also decide that the world is wrong, that some assets are "mispriced" and present trading opportunities for the shrewd investor. (p. xiii)

Any financial asset is, by definition, a package of cash flows in the form of deferred payments. The owner of a financial asset owns the right to receive all cash flows associated with the contract. A bond is a contract that gives the owner the right to receive coupons plus the final repayment of the principal; a firm's stock gives the owner the right to receive all future dividends plus the proceeds from the eventual final liquidation of the firm; an option gives the owner the right to receive a final payoff conditional on given events (in the case of stock call options, the payoff is equal to the difference between the market price of the underlying stock and the strike of the option); and so on for other financial contracts.

The price of financial assets is constrained by arguments about the absence of arbitrage. Consider the simplest case of a US government note with a nominal (face) value of $1,000 that matures in three years without coupons (i.e., a zero-coupon note). The theoretical price of the note is the present value of $1,000 discounted at the risk-free rate. The market price cannot be different from the theoretical price because this difference would create arbitrage opportunities. The price of any other government bond or note is also uniquely determined by the risk-free rates applicable to coupons (if any exist) and the principal. The reason is that US government bonds or notes are considered risk free; any other price would result in arbitrage opportunities. For example, in discrete time, assuming n periods, if the risk-free rate in period i is r_i, then the present value, PV, of a government bond with coupon C and principal M is

$$PV = \frac{C}{(1+r_1)} + \frac{C}{(1+r_1)(1+r_2)} + \cdots + \frac{C+M}{(1+r_1)(1+r_2)\cdots(1+r_n)}. \qquad (1)$$

Present value clearly depends on interest rates.

The supply of and demand for government bills (notes and bonds), as well as other financial assets, affects interest rates.[5] The supply of and demand for credit, as well as decisions made by central banks regarding the base rates, determine all risk-free rates. Interest rates can fluctuate greatly. For example, interest rates for US T-bills were below 1% in the immediate post–World War II period, soared to above 14% in the early 1980s, dropped to around 1% after the dot-com bubble, and then rose again, only to fall to below 1%—in fact, almost exactly zero—following the 2008 financial crisis. **Figure 1.1** represents three-month T-bill rates from 1934 to 2016. Supply and demand determine the term structure of interest rates, which in turn determine the price of every bill, note, and bond simultaneously.

Corporate bonds, unlike US government bonds, are subject to credit risk: The payment of coupons and repayment of the principal are uncertain because of the possibility of default and the percentage that can be recovered in case of default. So, in the case of corporate bonds, a bond's price is the sum of the *expected values* of coupons and of the principal, both discounted at a rate consisting of the risk-free rate plus a risk premium. Supply and demand contribute to the level of risk-free rates and determine—given the risk characteristics of each bond—the risk premium for that bond.

With stocks, the level of uncertainty is much higher than with bonds but the theoretical pricing framework is the same: Stock prices are the sum of the discounted values of expected cash flows. However, in the case of stocks, cash flows are not mandated by contract but are truly uncertain even if, in mature industries, the flow of dividends might be somewhat predictable and

---

[5]In modern monetary systems, the vast majority of money is created when agents take out loans. A study by Moore (1988) found that banks are not constrained by reserves in their lending. Contrary to the theory of the multiplier, he proposed a theory called Horizontalism by which money is created endogenously by the banking system in granting loans and simultaneously crediting the client's account. For a complete analysis of the modern process of money generation, see McLeay, Radia, and Thomas (2014a, 2014b).

Figure 1.1. Fluctuations of Three-Month T-Bill Rates, 1934–2016

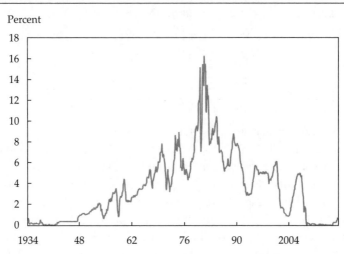

Source: Constructed by the authors using data obtained from Federal Reserve Economic Data Three-Month Treasury Bill: Secondary Market Rate.

the market valuation relatively stable. In addition, stocks are subject to risks other than solely credit risk.

The price of a firm's stock is (essentially) determined by expectations such as the ability of the firm to produce a steady flow of dividends and/or to command a high price in the future. In the absence of arbitrage opportunities, the market price of any financial asset is the sum of the expected discounted value of future cash flows. The discount rate is the risk-free rate plus a risk premium.

Discount rates for stocks are determined by the market—that is, by the interplay of supply and demand—and by the action of central banks and governments. Central banks determine the rate they pay on reserves—a basic interest rate that affects all other interest rates. Other considerations, including fiscal policies and risk regulations, affect all rates in the economy. The notion that assets' market prices are equal to the sum of expected discounted cash flows is general; it does not characterize the intrinsic price. In fact, prices can always be represented as the sum of expected discounted cash flows with appropriate discount rates.

To do the work that has traditionally been considered the job of an equity analyst and for which investment professionals are still widely considered to be paid (i.e., to "beat the market"), the profession tries to identify under- and overpriced assets and take advantage of that knowledge to realize a profit.

Doing so requires determining the intrinsic value of a stock, which in turn calls for determining the distribution of future cash flows, the true discount rates, and the risk premiums.

Much of the vast literature on stock valuation does not address this problem theoretically but devotes a lot of time to describing how to analyze a balance sheet and, eventually, how to forecast earnings or dividends. As for describing how to choose the discount rate, however, most authors simply recommend heuristics or historical values. The capital asset pricing model and factor models are also used.

That the concept of intrinsic value is tricky is not surprising. Even while considering intrinsic value central to investment management, the father of value investing, Benjamin Graham, found the concept "elusive" and cautioned against taking it as "definite and determinable" (Graham and Dodd, 1934; 2008 edition, p. 64). Marc Reinganum, a former senior managing director at State Street Global Advisors, commented on the elusive nature of intrinsic value:

> One should never confuse the concept of arbitrage (riskless profit) with intrinsic value. Intrinsic value always depends upon assumptions, and unless all investors always agree with these assumptions, there will never be one true value in practice. The best any one investor can hope for is that he or she understands the dynamics of stock prices a little bit better than most market participants.

In fact, the concept of the intrinsic value of financial assets depends on the possibility of defining a natural rate of return or, more correctly, a "natural rate of interest" plus a "natural risk premium." However, defining a natural rate of interest or a natural rate of return without recourse to macroeconomic considerations is well beyond the realm of pure finance theory. Macroeconomic considerations might shed new light on the question of market efficiency and the intrinsic value of stocks. The idea of a natural rate of interest was introduced by the Swedish economist Knut Wicksell (1898), who defined the natural rate of interest as that rate of interest that guarantees stable asset and consumer prices. We can think of a natural rate of interest as the equilibrium rate when market capitalization grows at the same rate as that of the economy.

The idea of a natural rate of interest returned to the fore of economic research after central banks accepted the notion of endogenous money generation and began to target interest rates, instead of the quantity of money, in the 1990s (see Bindseil and König 2013). Following the 2008 financial crisis, central banks lowered interest rates to what is sometimes called "the effective lower bound"—that is, zero—and began "unconventional" policies, such as quantitative easing (see McLeay, Radia, and Thomas 2014b). But, as years of prolonged near-zero interest rates by central banks failed to produce the desired economic growth, central bankers began to question just what the ideal interest rate should be.

If we could identify a rate of interest at which no excess demand for investments occurs, we might reasonably assume that we could identify the intrinsic value of assets as the price obtained by discounting cash flows with the natural rate of interest. Of course the problem of forecasting cash flows remains.

Central banks have developed models to compute the natural rate of interest. Lubik and Matthes (2015), from the US Federal Reserve Bank of Richmond, compared two approaches: (1) their approach, which uses a time-varying parameter vector autoregressive model, and (2) the Laubach–Williams model (see Laubach and Williams 2015), which uses a state–space approach.

The idea of a natural rate of interest is not without critics, who observe that no single rate of interest is able to guarantee stable prices and equilibrium between investments and savings.

The question of the natural rate of interest bears on the question of the relationship between stock returns and economic growth. Studying the period 1872–2014, Straehl and Ibbotson (2015) found that the increase of total payout (dividends plus share buybacks) follows the increase in per capita GDP over very long periods. Others, including Ritter (2005), have found no relationship (not even a negative relationship) between stock returns and economic growth. This question will be discussed in Chapter 4.

Following the notion that the intrinsic value of a financial asset is its price under some equilibrium condition led to a revision of the efficient market hypothesis (EMH). LeRoy (1976) was the first to point out that the original formulation of the EMH was a tautology.[6] In response to LeRoy, Fama (1976) introduced the idea that the true price is the price in economic equilibrium. More recently, Pilkington (2014) posited the idea that the EMH is really a hypothesis on an equilibrium situation of economies; that is, the EMH states that actual prices are equal to the prices of an economy where savings and investments are in equilibrium.

---

[6]In his 1970 paper, Fama (p. 384) suggested that markets are efficient if prices satisfy the following equation:

$$E(\tilde{p}_{j,t+1} \mid \Phi_t) = E\left[1 + (\tilde{r}_{j,t+1} \mid \Phi_t)\right] p_{j,t},$$

where $\tilde{p}_{j,t+1}$ and $\tilde{r}_{j,t+1}$ are prices and returns at time $t+1$ anticipated at time t and Φ_t is the information set at time t. LeRoy (1976) observed that this equation is a tautology because the expectation of prices at time $t+1$ with the information set at time t is *by definition* equal to prices at time t multiplied by the expectation of returns at time $t+1$.

The conceptual underpinning of intrinsic value as outlined here shows that the notion of intrinsic value is neither easy to understand nor easy to apply. The intrinsic value of a financial asset would be the price of that financial asset in a different economy. In fact, there are a number of questions:

- Is fundamental (or intrinsic) value more than an intellectual construct?

- Is intrinsic value based on empirical data?

- Can intrinsic value be determined with the tools financial analysts presently have?

- If intrinsic value is no more than an intellectual concept or if the quest to determine intrinsic value proves elusive, why not limit our quest to determining a stock's value as its market (or fair) value with the use of heuristics such as market multiples or rules such as what has become known as the Buffett Rule, which states that markets are over-/undervalued as a function of the ratio between market capitalization and GDP?[7]

- Or why not simply turn to alternative methods—for example, pattern or trend analysis—which might improve one's chances of realizing gains?

That the "true" price of an investment can be realized only under a hypothetical situation of equilibrium is not obvious. Equity analysts might find it difficult to compute the interest rates that apply to these elusive states of equilibrium of savings and investments. And how can we be sure that the economy will revert to a situation of equilibrium? How long will doing so take?

In commenting on the concept of intrinsic value, Alfred Slager, a professor of pension fund management at the TIAS School for Business and Society at Tilburg University and a trustee at the Dutch pension fund for general practitioners SPH, said,

> I view the concept of intrinsic value mainly as an intellectual construct. It's very useful for understanding the building blocks of a stock market but rather difficult to build successful investment strategies on. Determining the value of the underlying company is tricky enough, but with the advances in real options theory, etc., it seems rather robust.
>
> On the other hand, the linkage between the intrinsic value and valuation of a stock has not really made any progress in my view, and probably never

---

[7]The accuracy of this rule is subject to changes in the amount of equity risk in a given economy that is publicly traded. For example, in the 1980s, Germany appeared to be undervalued, but that appearance was because the equities were held privately by families, while corporate debt was held by banks.

will. The notion that there might be a fundamental or intrinsic value in a stock seems to me a remainder of the idea that we could/might apply general equilibrium models to the stock market. What we know is that there is supply and demand, which determines a stock's price. The residual value (or multiple), the gap between the stock price and intrinsic value, is then more or less determined at random.

I readily admit that's a dismal view, and one which we do not accept as a sector. We construct models to explain this gap, and because we use similar models and base our buy-and-sell advice on these models, on a large scale we might find that there exists a correlation between the valuation models and the multiple, but that is induced by market behavior and has little to do with fundamental analysis.

Things simplify considerably if we drop the notion of intrinsic price and try to establish only relative pricing valuations. In other words, we might simply ask whether the ordering of market prices corresponds to the ordering of intrinsic prices. This question is much simpler and can be answered without a precise knowledge of natural rates of interest or natural risk premiums. Relative market evaluations depend, at least in first approximation, on estimates of the distribution of future cash flows. In practice, these valuations can be done with fundamental analysis, without forecasting. The crucial question is, Does the process of discovering the intrinsic price allow better returns? Somehow, the market price has to be tied to the intrinsic price to understand whether situations of nonequilibrium, such as bubbles, are developing.

2. Tools for Valuing Stocks: Intrinsic Value and Relative Value

In the previous chapter, we explored theoretical questions related to the valuation of a firm's shares and, specifically, the notion of intrinsic value in a free market based on supply and demand. In particular, we discussed how determining the intrinsic value of a stock implies determining the interest rates and risk premiums in a situation of market equilibrium. In practice, however, the notion of intrinsic price is used for relative comparisons and for evaluating situations of strong disequilibrium. In other words, evaluating whether a stock is cheap or expensive with respect to other stocks is possible, but evaluating whether a stock is cheap or expensive in absolute is not, except in situations far from conditions of equilibrium.

Let's now take a look at the tools investment professionals use to estimate a stock's value. We will start with tools to discover the intrinsic value of a firm's stock. The CFA Institute Survey of the equity valuation practices of its members, "Equity Valuation: A Survey of Professional Practice" (Pinto, Robinson, and Stowe 2015), had the objective of documenting professional practice in the selection of equity valuation approaches. The survey also asked whether a specific tool was viewed by the analyst as widely or narrowly applicable. A mean frequency of greater than 50% would suggest that the tool was viewed as a general tool, and a mean frequency of less than 50% would indicate that use of the tool was limited to special cases.[8]

The survey found (see **Table 2.1**) that among the absolute valuation models used to determine the intrinsic value of a firm, nearly 80% of the survey participants reported that they use a discounted present value approach. Slightly more than 60% reported using an asset-based approach, but a lower mean frequency (just under 37%) indicates that its use is more restricted. Note that a market multiples approach, which we will discuss later, is the most widely used valuation method among participants.

Jarrod Wilcox, president of Wilcox Investment, commented on the use of various models in equity valuation, saying,

> A particular valuation model may be useful for one purpose and not for another. For example, the cyclically adjusted price–earnings ratio (CAPE)

---

[8]A total of 1,980 practitioners in the Americas (66% of the total), Asia Pacific (12% of the total), and Europe, the Middle East, and Africa (22% of the total) participated in the CFA Institute Survey (Pinto et al. 2015).

Table 2.1. Most Widely Used Valuation Approaches among Respondents to the 2015 CFA Institute Study

Valuation Approaches: Global ranking. In evaluating individual equity securities, which of the following approaches to valuation do you use? $N = 1,980$	Percentage of Respondents	Percentage of Cases in Which the Respondent Uses Each of the Approaches[a] (mean)
A market multiples approach	92.8	68.6
A discounted present value approach	78.8	59.5
An asset-based approach	61.4	36.8
A (real) options approach	5.0	20.7
Other approach	12.7	58.1

[a]Respondents using an approach were asked for the percentage of valuation cases in which the approach is used. Thus, this column reports conditional frequencies.
Source: CFA Institute.

model is good for long-term forecasts of aggregate US stock market returns but not so useful for stock return forecasts in the shorter term, for cross-sectional explanations of price, or for corporate CEOs interested in the easiest way to enhance the value of their company. Another example is the dividend discount model, which helps us organize our thoughts but is weak in forecasting future returns. How do we measure future dividends today?

Net Present Value Models

Models used to compute net present value (NPV) require two key steps: (1) the forecasting of future cash flows and (2) the estimation of discount factors—that is, the risk-free rate plus a risk premium. Forecasts of future cash flows are based on the fundamental analysis of a firm plus models of future projections of cash flows and their uncertainty. As discussed in Chapter 1, the intrinsic discount factor cannot really be determined without macroeconomic considerations, including knowledge of the financial and banking system.

In practice, however, analysts use various techniques for making a reasonable estimate of a required rate of return (equivalent to the discount rate if the market is in equilibrium). The required rate of return is the benchmark return rate used by investors in their decision-making process. If, on the one hand, the expected return of a stock is higher than the required rate, then the stock is considered underpriced and is a candidate for investment; if, on the other hand, the expected return is lower than the required return, the stock is considered overpriced and therefore not a good candidate for investment.

Discounted present value approaches use company fundamentals to try to determine the intrinsic value of a firm, in which the value is the sum of discounted expected future cash flows. Two basic versions of this model are used: the dividend discount model (DDM) and the discounted cash flow (DCF) model. In the DDM, dividends are considered the relevant cash flows. But dividends are discretionary, which makes their forecasting problematic. In fact, one has to forecast not only how the company will perform but also the decisions that will be made about the distribution of dividends (versus reinvestment of profits into the company's operations). For this reason, many prefer DCF models, which use a different concept of the company's discounted future cash flows.

The idea behind a DCF model is that what is important is the cash available, regardless of whether or not it is distributed. An advantage of DCF is its applicability to listed and unlisted companies alike. The limits of these models are well known: A DDM can be used only in cases where a firm pays stable (and predictable) dividends; the DCF, only in cases where a firm has positive (and predictable) free cash flows. ("Free" cash flow equals cash flow minus an allowance for enough reinvestment of cash to keep the company in a steady state, by replacing equipment and so forth.)

Among the investment academics and professionals with whom we spoke, most prefer (free) cash flow models. The insight here: The price of a stock reflects the expectations of future cash flows. Christian Kjaer, head of global equities and volatility at Denmark's largest pension provider ATP ($113 billion in assets under management), commented, "All models shed light on some aspect of 'the truth'; they all have their pros and cons. However, on the margin, we favor the free-cash-flow model, basically because we find free cash flows less prone to manipulation."

Kenneth Little, managing director of the investments group at Brandes Investment Partners, made a similar evaluation:

> We believe that most or all financial models used to determine the fundamental value of a firm's stock are essentially shortcuts to a full discounted free cash flow valuation of a firm. While all valuation models have their respective shortfalls and are very sensitive to underlying assumptions, to the extent they are long-term in nature, focused on free cash flow, and appropriately risk adjusted, these models represent a reasonable methodology for approximating a firm's fundamental value.

Bradford Cornell, professor of financial economics at the California Institute of Technology, also favors the cash flow model: "Ultimately, it is the expected future cash flow that determines value. The stock market is the mechanism by which those expectations get reflected in price."

Fundamental equity portfolios at PGGM Investments, the Dutch pension fund with €189 billion in assets under management, are constructed on the basis of fundamental models—in particular, DCF models. Felix Lanters, head of equities there, said,

> We consider discounted cash flow models to be the better of models—if there is such a thing—for gaining a fair assessment of the long-term ability of the firm to generate profits. Our objective is not to obtain a single price but clarity on how the valuation resets in changing assumptions. As with any model, you need to make a lot of assumptions, but the free cash flow model allows you to change assumptions, create scenarios, and find sensitivity to fluctuations. For example, if relatively small changes in a single factor have a big impact on valuation, this raises red flags. We use the free cash model very broadly, with more reflection of the underlying processes as opposed to just looking at what comes out of the model.

Matteo Bonaventura, a buy-side financial analyst at Banor SIM in Milan, also finds the scenario-like properties of the DCF model a plus. He remarked,

> I think that the most interesting aspect of DCF models is sensitivity analysis, as it provides some sort of confidence interval for your estimates. Moreover, it can provide some interesting insights. For example, the change in estimated intrinsic value to changes in the cost of capital can be interpreted as a raw proxy of the equity duration—that is, the sensitivity of equity prices to changes in interest rates.

Although he uses both DDM and DCF models, Bonaventura prefers the DCF model for most companies.

For estimating the intrinsic value of an investment, Sébastien Lleo, who has nine years of experience in financial markets and is now a finance professor at NEOMA Business School (France), also prefers discounted free-cash-flow (DFCF) models—namely DFCF to the firm and to equity—and adjusted present value methodologies, methods he links to John Burr Williams's (1938) pioneering work on investment management. However, he has some reservations:

> In theory, this class of models provides the most accurate valuation. In practice, however, their valuation is sensitive to the choice of inputs and their underlying assumptions (equity risk premium, annual sales growth, long-term growth, exit multiple, …). When the choice of input is often subjective, the model output becomes subjective as well. To summarize this situation, we could rephrase the expression "garbage in, garbage out," familiar to optimization professionals as "subjective in, subjective out." This means that free-cash-flow methodologies are only truly meaningful when they are complemented by sensitivity analysis and scenario analysis. The true virtue

of these methods is, therefore, to provide a range of possible valuations under a variety of scenarios, not a point estimate.

Bonaventura added another critique—not of the DDM or DCF models themselves but of their application:

Many times, there is the risk that DCF becomes a back-of-the-envelope exercise—that is, you start from an idea of target price and you adjust numbers to make it happen. Moreover, many times, DCF is applied incorrectly from a theoretical point of view—for example, when applying constant cost of capital rates or in the application of the perpetual growth rates. Empirical evidence is reported by Professor Fernandez.[9]

Slager offered a somewhat different view, saying,

I find that when I teach these models, they resonate far better in the corporate finance–related courses than in [investment] finance. With corporate finance, they offer students insights into the drivers of the *value* of a corporation. For investment students, they are insights in the *valuation* of a corporation. Personally, I find that the DDM models are more relevant for the stock market and free-cash-flow models more related to corporate finance.

Ananth Madhavan, the global head of research, exchange-traded funds, and index investments at BlackRock and a lecturer on financial engineering at the Haas School of Business at the University of California, Berkeley, noted, "Many practitioners combine other approaches with DCF by using comparable firm multiples to find a more robust estimate of terminal value that takes into account maturity."

The challenge in using present value models is the dependence of future cash flows on, and the predictability of, input forecasts, such as a company's return on invested capital, its growth rate, and its weighted average cost of capital. The key difficulty is in forecasting future dividends, cash flows, and the discount rate.

In theory, both the DDM and DCF models include an infinite stream of cash flows and/or the eventual final liquidation of the firm. In practice, however, all models make forecasts of dividends or cash flows over a finite time horizon, typically 5 to 10 years. Therefore, every present value model, in practice, has two components: the present value of cash flows before the time horizon and the terminal value at the time horizon.

The terminal value at the time horizon is a particularly critical issue. Penman (2016) writes,

Finite-horizon forecasts of dividends typically do not capture value. … In short, dividends are zero-NPV. Thus, forecasting dividends is of no help

---

[9]This reference is to Fernandez (2015).

17

in establishing value (the case of a firm that "pays no dividends" being an extreme example). (p. 6)

The relative worth of the terminal value with respect to the total value is, therefore, an important issue. Charles Lee (2005), professor of accounting at the Graduate School of Business at Stanford University and cofounder of San Francisco–based Nipun Capital, observes that the terminal value depends on the maturity of the firm and the sector. He notes that in a mature sector (such as the tobacco industry), over an eight-year time horizon, the terminal value represents 56% of the total; in the skin care sector, the terminal value represents the totality of the present value; and in the high-tech sector, the first eight years of a firm yield negative cash flows, and the terminal value might represent 125% of the total present value.

Lee remarks that there is in fact a progressive shift from models such as the DDM or DCF model to the residual income model (RIM), a model based more on value creation than on cash distribution. He observes that over the entire life of a firm, wealth creation must equal the sum of dividends paid. Over short time horizons, however, wealth creation differs from dividends paid. The residual income is the income generated in a given period minus the cost of capital needed to generate that income. The RIM values a company at a given time by computing the present value of future residual income plus the capital of the firm.

In addition to evaluating cash flows, the other crucial element in present value models is the discount rate. As observed in Chapter 1, determining the intrinsic value of a stock is somehow equivalent to identifying a *natural* rate of interest and a *natural* rate of return. Both are related to a situation of macroeconomic equilibrium where prices are stable, there is full employment, and the money available for investment equals the money needed for investment.

The problem of determining the intrinsic value of stocks is, therefore, the problem of determining an equilibrium economic situation. Central banks in the biggest economies have become increasingly interested in the problem of determining the natural interest rate because, in the aftermath of the 2008 financial crisis, the policies of central banks have been focused on setting interest rates.

Among the more popular models for determining the natural interest rate is the Laubach–Williams model. Laubach and Williams (2015) state,

> The natural rate is assumed to depend on the estimated contemporaneous trend growth rate of potential output and a time-varying unobserved component that captures the effects of other unspecified influences on the natural rate. In mathematical terms, the natural rate of interest, denoted r_t^* is given by: $r_t^* = c + g_t^* + z_t$, where g_t^* is the estimated trend growth rate of potential GDP, z_t is an unobserved component that is assumed to follow a

random walk process, and c is an estimated coefficient that measures the influence of the trend growth rate on the natural rate of interest.

The model is estimated using the Kalman filter.[10]

This and similar models are still largely ignored in the finance literature on the DCF and DDM models, where no mention is made of how to measure the discount factor. Talking about models makes little sense if the critical component of the model—the discount factor—cannot be identified. In fact, most of the investment and finance literature simply assumes that rates read off the US Treasury curve are the correct riskless rates for discounting.

Penman (2016) discusses this problem, writing,

> Modern finance has struggled with the question of the discount rate—the cost of capital—producing the Capital Asset Pricing Model (CAPM) and subsequent multi-factor models. Again based on no-arbitrage, the structure of a generalized "asset pricing model" is understood, in the form of common return factors (the risk of which cannot be diversified away) and sensitivity to those factors. However, operational identification of those factors has proved elusive, let alone sensitivities to the unidentified factors. (p. 6)

In addition to the problem of forecasting related to the use of any present value model, there are other problems. Consider, for example, the DDM and corporate share buybacks. For the full year 2016, Standard & Poor's (S&P 2017) announced that firms in the S&P 500 spent $536.4 billion on buybacks, whereas for the period 2009–2016, S&P 500 firms repurchased $2.75 trillion in stock. Another figure comes from Birinyi Associates, which estimates that US-listed companies spent about $6.1 trillion buying back their own shares during the 11-year period 2005–2016.[11]

Buybacks have two effects. First, by increasing demand for a stock, buybacks increase the stock price, thereby increasing the realized risk premium. Second, buybacks reduce the amount of cash available to pay dividends; many researchers regard them as a substitute for dividends, an alternative way of returning cash to the shareholder. Cornell at the California Institute of Technology commented that, given corporate buybacks and other innovations, dividend models are less useful than they once were. Philip Straehl, a senior research consultant and portfolio manager at Morningstar Investment Management, and Roger Ibbotson, the chairman and chief investment officer (CIO) of Zebra Capital Management and a Yale School of Management professor, agree. They argue (Straehl and Ibbotson 2015) that the shift in

---

[10]The Kalman filter is a technique for estimating hidden variables in linear systems.
[11]We thank Birinyi's Chris Costelleo for providing us with this information in an Excel spreadsheet.

corporate payout policy from dividends to buybacks has caused a "secular decrease in dividend yields, and an analogous increase in per-share growth" (p. 25). This, they add, has led to "a structural break in the return components of the traditional supply models such as the dividend discount model" (p. 25), creating the need for a new supply model of stock returns.

Straehl and Ibbotson (2015) propose such a model, which they call the "total payout" model of stock returns. Their total-payout model includes both dividends and buybacks: It is based on computing separately the extra return that investors enjoy as a result of buybacks. The authors regard the sum of dividends and buybacks as the reward to investors for "participating in the real economy" through share ownership.

Hence, we have another important question. Straehl and Ibbotson (2015) define the "total payout of stocks" as the sum of dividends plus the cash payout resulting from buybacks. They found that over the 142-year period 1872–2014, the total payout per share and the per capita GDP of the United States grew at approximately the same rate, albeit with large fluctuations (we will discuss this phenomenon more in Chapter 4). They argue that their total-payout model allows for good forecasts of long-term stock returns.

BlackRock's Madhavan, in contrast, believes that the effect of buybacks on the risk premium is ambiguous:

> Buybacks offer an alternative (and perhaps more tax-efficient) way of distributing cash to shareholders than paying dividends. In the frictionless, symmetric information, and tax-free world of Miller and Modigliani, the value of the firm is the same in both cases, although the stock price with a buyback is higher than when a dividend is paid. Any changes in expected returns then reflect real-world frictions such as signaling effects. Consequently, practitioners often condition on the type of buyback—for example, whether it is a share repurchase program, tender offer, etc.—and the context for the buyback—for example, related to earnings or corporate events.

Other present value methods include an asset-based approach (used by 61% of the CFA Institute Survey participants, with a mean frequency of 37%) and a (real) options approach (used by 5% of the CFA Institute Survey participants, with a mean frequency of 21%). These approaches are clearly more narrowly applicable than the DDM and DCF models.

Asset-based valuation is used in various contexts—in particular, in cases where valuation does not depend on income. One example is liquidation. In this case, assets are valued at the market price at which they could be sold. Still, certain intangibles, such as a brand name, can be sold on the basis of their potential to generate future income.

Asset-based valuation is also used in other cases, such as when balance sheets need to be rectified so that each item reflects its current value or when a value must be assigned to various parts of a business in preparation for the purchase or sale of some part of the business. In this last case, the valuation of each asset item follows the same principle as the valuation of the entire business. The intrinsic value method can be used by computing the present value of each item based on its ability to generate cash; alternatively, relative valuation methods can be used to value an asset by comparison with similar assets.

Relative Valuation and Market Multiples

As discussed previously, the NPV approach suffers from some significant conceptual difficulties—not least in defining the asset's intrinsic price. When the use of a discounted present value approach is deemed difficult or inappropriate, relative valuation methods based on heuristics—in particular, market multiples—are the tools of choice. As the name implies, market multiples are tools to determine the price of an asset relative to the price of a similar (comparable) asset. So, they establish a ranking of asset values.

Referring again to the CFA Institute Survey, we note that a market multiples approach is the mostly widely used of all valuation techniques: Almost 93% of the survey participants reported that they use multiplier models, which are considered general valuation tools (see Table 2.1). The most widely used market multiples (see **Table 2.2**) are the P/E multiple (used by 88%) and enterprise value (EV)—in particular, EV/EBITDA (used by 77%), followed by price-to-book (59%) and price-to-(some measure of) cash flow (57%).

Commenting on market multiples, Banor SIM's Bonaventura said,

> I find that relative valuation models are very useful in the everyday activity of stock evaluation. However, the analysis needs to be integrated with more understanding of the multiple and of why companies are trading at a premium or a discount. Given that two companies are similar, multiples can be a first tool to screen for economic attractiveness. While I don't think that multiples are able to anticipate stock returns, in my opinion they can be a useful tool when considered in aggregate for sectors or the whole market. For example, if reverse engineered, they can provide quick and useful information on the current level of the risk premium.

At Brandes Investment Partners, Little remarked,

> We believe relative valuation models provide a reasonable method to determine how firms are valued relative to one another, but they do little to help forecast future equity returns on an absolute basis. There are numerous

Table 2.2. Most Widely Used Market Multiples Approach among Respondents to the 2015 CFA Institute Study

Market Multiples Approach: When you use a market multiples approach, which of the following ratios do you use? N = 1,765	Percentage of Respondents	Percentage of Cases in Which the Respondent Uses Each of the Approaches (mean)
D/P (dividend yield) or P/D (price-to-dividend)	35.5	44.3
Enterprise value (EV) or firm value multiples (e.g., EV-to-EBITDA, EV-to-operating profit)	76.7	61.1
P/B (price-to-book value, price-to-adjusted book value, book-to-market)	59.0	44.8
P/CF (price to some measure of cash flow)	57.2	54.6
P/S (price-to-sales or revenues)	40.3	45.7
P/E (price to some measure of earnings)	88.1	67.2
Other ratios	11.6	58.5

Source: CFA Institute.

historical examples of firms that were "relatively" undervalued compared to their peers but generated poor future equity returns because the entire peer group was overvalued. And conversely, it can be the case that a firm may generate attractive long-term equity returns despite its value appearing expensive relative to its peers. The more a market is mispriced, the less pertinent relative valuation models would appear to be.

Eric Sorensen, president and chief executive at Boston-based PanAgora Asset Management, commented on the firm's approach to P/E valuation for US stock selection:

Our processes for US stocks excluded the use of P/E ratios prior to the 2005–2007 bubble in quant equity. We consider that P/E has two flaws: (1) one size fits all is too crude, and (2) P/E is ubiquitous in free datasets. Advanced and actionable relative value calculations for sectors and stocks must be specific to the businesses of the firms. P/E ratios are too abundant and have been arbitraged away for 15 years. Our work, as examples, includes (1) for financials, valuing the risk of the cash flows for the specific loan or contract portfolios using default signals that adjust the discount specific rates and (2) for biotech, valuing—with an option theoretic approach—the probabilistic potential of the specific drugs undergoing FDA [US Food and Drug Administration] test-phase trials using Markov chain models.

Multiples are not used at all at PGGM Investments. Lanters commented,

> We consider multiples a distraction from what is important—that is to say, real valuation. Multiples are a one-dimensional measurement. A rather silly idea: The P or the E is low, high. It does not matter if the multiple is high if the present value is low compared to the share price.

Pablo Fernandez (2002), a professor of financial management at the University of Navarra's IESE Business School, gives a more fundamental critique of equity valuation methods. Fernandez considers that all methods other than DCF methods, though used, are not in accord with finance theory.

As mentioned previously, relative valuations are not exempt from some of the conceptual difficulties of absolute valuations. Here's why: Consider the most widely used relative asset valuation tool, the P/E. Ultimately, the strongest formulation of the P/E principle states that an intrinsic, natural ratio exists between the price of a stock and its earnings and that this ratio is universal. To allow for random fluctuations, we can state that for each asset the following relationship holds:

$$P = \left(\frac{P}{E}\right)E + \varepsilon, \tag{2}$$

where P is the price of the stock, E represents the earnings per share, and ε is random noise. Let's leave unanswered for the moment the question of the timeframe over which we compute E. If a true intrinsic P/E exists, then Equation 2 would allow us to understand whether the stock is cheap or expensive.

But determining a natural, intrinsic P/E is akin to determining a natural rate of return. Sometimes the average P/E of a market is compared with a historical average of the P/E of the same market. **Figure 2.1** shows the cross-sectional average P/E for the S&P 500 for the 146-year period 1871–2017.

As can be seen from Figure 2.1, for this 146-year period, the P/E had a mean of 15.64, with values as low as 5.31 (December 1917) and as high as 123.73 (May 2009, truncated in the graph). In the two most recent decades, not only did the P/E increase, but fluctuations in the ratio also grew. Clearly, considering the 146-year average (15.64) a natural benchmark is problematic.

Given these difficulties and the fact that stocks in different sectors often exhibit considerably different P/Es, in using a multiples approach, analysts typically create small groups of similar (comparable) firms. A multiples

Figure 2.1. The Cross-Sectional P/E for the S&P 500 and Predecessor Indexes, 1871–2017

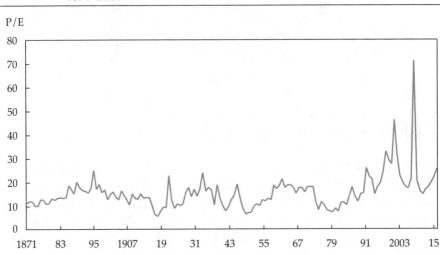

Source: Constructed by the authors using data obtained from www.multpl.com/table.

valuation process is thus dependent on the selection of comparable firms (that is, firms with similar growth patterns and returns on capital and subject to the same macroeconomic forces) and their respective pricing.

Shiller's cyclically adjusted P/E (CAPE) is a variant of the P/E that takes a 10-year average of earnings as the basis for looking at current pricing levels (see Siegel 2016). The popularity of the P/E comes from its focus on earnings. EPS is a major component in the P/E valuation. Although EPS is generally considered a primary driver of value—determinant of a share's price—some analysts believe EPS can be easily manipulated by, for example, share buybacks, as mentioned in our discussion of the DDM.

Fabozzi, Chen, Ma, and West (2015) started with the research question: Given the wide mistrust in measures of earnings, why are earnings so widely used as a financial metric—as opposed to, for example, cash flow? The authors remark,

> The stock market has an unusual fascination with earnings. A company's earnings, measured under specific accounting standards and tax laws, are arbitrary at best, whereas cash flow, like the balance in a checking account, is an actual number and subject to little interpretation. In practice, a company could file for bankruptcy while showing positive net earnings but negative cash flows on its financial statements. (p. 511)

Using a sample of US stocks from CRSP[12] for the 1970–2014 period, the authors performed an empirical study to determine the sensitivity of prices to a number of factors and concluded,

> Stock prices are, on average, affected by short-term earnings. … We find that cash flow pricing is used primarily to price what we classify as "negative" stocks—stocks that are generally characterized as illiquid, mispriced, or having a shorter trading history, negative earnings, or negative market performance. Thus, the practice appears to collide with modern finance theories. (p. 511)

Nevertheless, the authors consider the wide use of earnings rational: The use of earnings is part of conforming to the majority.

The CAPE model—or rather, the data used to estimate the model when valuing US equities—was the subject of a recent critique by Jeremy Siegel (2016), professor of finance at the Wharton School of the University of Pennsylvania. Siegel suggests that even though CAPE is among the best forecasting models for long-term future stock returns, the CAPE model is "overpessimistic" (p. 41) in its return forecasts because of changes in the way GAAP earnings used in the model are calculated.[13] He advocates using National Income and Product Account after-tax corporate profits to estimate the model. This approach, Siegel believes, will result in higher explanatory power and significantly higher stock return forecasts.

This idea raises a general question regarding the input data when using multiples: Do we use trailing or forward-looking multiples? A trailing multiple is a multiple based on historical data; a forward-looking multiple is a multiple computed on forecast data. Value investors, including Benjamin Graham and Warren Buffett, prefer historical data. Janet Lowe (2010) reports that Buffett commented, "I have no use whatsoever for projections or forecasts. They create an illusion of apparent precision. The more meticulous they are, the more concerned you should be. We never look at projections, but we care very much about, and look very deeply at, track records."

A problem with using historical data is that for a firm whose earnings change rapidly, the measure will lag.

A problem with using future market multiples is the universal problem with forecasts—that they may be inaccurate. In their 2002 paper, however, Liu, Nissim, and Thomas report that forward earnings measures using

---

[12]CRSP is the Center for Research in Security Prices at the University of Chicago Booth School of Business.
[13]GAAP is a standard framework of guidelines for financial accounting used in Canada, the United Kingdom, and the United States.

one-year or two-year forecasted earnings perform better than historical earnings measures. Using a sample of companies trading on the New York Stock Exchange, the American Stock Exchange, and NASDAQ, they found that forward-looking measures are generally more accurate predictors of value than historical measures. P/Es based on forecasts of income (net and operating) were preferred by slightly more than 81% of the participants in the CFA Institute Survey of Professional Practice (Pinto et al. 2015), and trailing P/Es (net and operating) by just over 13%.

Robeco Institutional Asset Management (2016), an Amsterdam-based asset manager with €137 billion under management, says CAPE is its preferred approach to valuing stocks but has found the original Shiller CAPE to be United States specific; it has therefore constructed a worldwide measure. Although Robeco uses historical data, it has found that CAPE's predictive ability remains good compared with other valuation measures.

The debate about whether to use historical data or projected data is ultimately ill conceived. By nature, every financial decision is forward looking—that is, based on forecasts. Even if investors use historical data, they make projections. The question is not whether to make projections but *how* to do so. Analysts might forecast ratios and choose portfolios on the basis of forecasts of ratios or portfolio returns; that is, they might choose portfolios on the basis of current or past ratios.

Before we make additional observations about the valuation methods discussed here, we want to mention another heuristic popular in valuations—the ratio of the percentage of total market capitalization to the GNP or GDP of the relevant country. This ratio is often referred to as the Buffett ratio because Warren Buffett told *Fortune* magazine journalist Carol Loomis (2001) that he considers it likely "the best single measure of where valuations stand at any given moment." This ratio concerns aggregate equity returns, however, not individual stocks; we will examine this issue in Chapter 4 in the discussion of fair value and price distortions.

Valuation Methods Compared

"Beware of value illusion," warns Steven Greiner, senior vice president at Charles Schwab's Equity Ratings Department and author of *Ben Graham Was a Quant: Raising the IQ of the Intelligent Investor* (2011), who says, "A value trap is a stock that looks underappreciated by the market as measured by typical relative valuation measures but in reality is low priced for good, fundamental business reasons and is a value illusion." Although our intention here is not to provide a review of the numerous texts on the issue of valuation methods, we will mention briefly some academic studies that show a variety of opinions on these methods' usefulness. Let's look first at the question of present value models.

In "Valuation: The State of the Art," Penman (2016) critiques standard valuation models from three points of view: accordance with the established theory of finance, practicality of use, and accounting methods and data used. In introducing the subject, Penman writes,

> There is a pervasive skepticism about formal valuation models, so much so that practitioners often discard them, preferring rough-cut methods such as pricing on the basis of comparables or simple P/E ratios. (p. 3)

As mentioned previously, although market multiples are the most widely used valuation methods, they are considered by some to be less relevant than present value models because they are only relative pricing measures: They inform on the value of an asset relative to that of other assets, not the intrinsic value of the asset. Behind their use is the belief that markets will eventually identify and correct "mispricings." In other words, the use of multiples allows an analyst to forecast future price movements of a given stock. Multiples can also be used to forecast earnings. If the analyst knows the multiple and assumes that it will not change in the forecasting horizon, the analyst can forecast prices by forecasting earnings.

In a note to business executives on the use of multiples, McKinsey consultants Goedhart, Koller, and Wessels (2005) cite several ways by which multiples can mislead. Their list includes (1) the difficulty in selecting truly comparable firms within the same sector, (2) the fact that different multiples can suggest conflicting conclusions, and (3) the idea that not all multiples are meaningful in various contexts.

What value measures are good forecasters of performance? Wilcox commented,

> It is worth repeating that a good model of the current price as a function of balance sheet, income statement, and cash flow statement may accurately forecast convergence between future model values and prices for an ensemble of firms but be of very little use in forecasting relative returns. The convergence may come either because values change—poor accounting is one reason (the future may reflect facts known but not in the accounting for valid reasons)—or prices change, and only the latter indicates possible mispricing and enhanced returns.

In the academic literature, a number of authors have contributed to the fundamental question of what value measures are good forecasters of future performance. Stanford University's Lee (2003) offers a review of criteria for choosing a valuation approach. He begins by observing that valuation methods can be either relative or direct. Relative valuation methods include all ratios, while direct methods include the balance sheet approach, the contingent claims approach, and the cash forecast approach.

Lee notes that the balance sheet approach does not consider intangibles and the contingent claims approach has many problems in estimation; he thus focused on cash flow methods. According to Lee, these methods are similar and yield similar results:

> A forecast-cash-flow approach encompasses various derivatives of the dividend discount model (DDM), such as the DCF model, the Edwards–Bell–Ohlson (EBO) model, the economic value added (EVA) model, and the residual income model (RIM). All of these models are essentially the same; like different brands of camera, they work the same way. (p. 5)

Lee believes that these models are conceptually sound but observes that they require the evaluation of three key elements: cash flows, terminal value, and discount rates. As for discount rates, as we noted in Chapter 1, evaluating them is more than an estimation problem: It is a conceptual problem. Estimating cash flows involves judgment. Lee notes that we cannot separate forecasting cash flows and forecasting terminal value. The specific notion of terminal value that we adopt is linked to the notion of cash flow that we adopt. The two go together.

Moving to multiples, Lee observes that the choice of multiples goes together with the choice of peers:

> Multiples are simple to apply as a valuation tool, but valuations derived from multiples can be subjective. That is not to say that a DCF model will not produce a subjective valuation, but the key to a good multiple-based approach is a judicious selection of peers. (p. 10)

Lee recommends the use of fundamental analysis to determine the group of peers and their median values. Warranted multiples are those multiples that apply to companies preselected with standard valuation tools. The key takeaway: the multiples approach works well if the peer group is correctly chosen.

Gray and Vogel (2012) performed a thorough analysis of various ratios: earnings to market capitalization (E/M), EBITDA to total enterprise value (EBITDA/TEV), free cash flow to total enterprise value (FCF/TEV), gross profits to total enterprise value (GP/TEV), book value to market value (B/M), and forward earnings estimates to market capitalization (FE/M)—all expressed in yield format—for the 1971–2010 period. They found that relative to other valuation metrics, EBITDA/TEV is the best valuation metric to use as an investment strategy. Eliminating stocks below the 10% NYSE market–equity breakpoint, they found that for the period under study, an annually rebalanced equal-weighted portfolio of high-EBITDA/TEV stocks earned annual returns of 17.66%, with a 2.91% annual three-factor alpha. Gray and Vogel concluded that this measure compares favorably with E/M; cheap-E/M stocks earned 15.23% a year.

Actually, an equal-weighted portfolio is, in itself, a good active strategy. DeMiguel, Garlappi, and Uppal (2009) claim that the equal-weighted portfolio is very difficult to beat.

In the aforementioned Gray and Vogel study, the authors also observe that value-weighted portfolios exhibit similar results, though returns are smaller than those of equal-weighted portfolios. This result is reasonable given that equal-weighted portfolios take advantage of the relative mean-reverting behavior of stocks. Interestingly, they also found that using forward estimates based on analysts' consensus yields produced the worst performance.

Some, including McKinsey's corporate finance practice in New York, consider the P/E—ubiquitous as it is—distorted in its traditional form by differences in capital structure and other nonoperating items, such as restructuring charges and write-offs. They advise using EV/EBITA or EV/EBITDA, the most widely used market multiples after P/E, according to participants in the 2015 CFA Institute Survey (see Pinto et al. 2015). McKinsey's Nolen Foushee, Koller, and Mehta (2012) believe that these multiples do not suffer from distortions that affect earnings ratios. Nevertheless, they write,

> Comparisons based on enterprise-value multiples typically reveal a very narrow range of peer-company multiples. A closer look at the US consumer-packaged-goods industry is illustrative. From 1965 to 2010, the difference in EV/EBITA multiples between top- and bottom-quartile companies was, for the most part, less than four points, even though the industry is fairly diverse, including companies that manufacture and sell everything from household cleaners to soft drinks.
>
> When we examined more closely matched peers at a given point in time, we found even narrower ranges: for a sample of branded-food companies, for example, EV/EBITA multiples ranged from 10.6 to 11.4. For medical-device companies, the range was 8.4 to 9.7. In ranges this narrow, any differences between true peers at a given point in time are typically unremarkable. A company's position in the ranking is likely to be quite variable simply as a result of normal share-price fluctuations. (p. 3)

In two papers, Liu, Nissim, and Thomas (2002, 2007) looked at the relative performance of multiples. In their 2002 paper, they studied multiples as variables for forecasting market prices in the US market. Examining the valuation performance of a comprehensive list of value drivers, they found that multiples derived from forward earnings explain stock prices remarkably well. Pricing errors were within 15% of stock prices for roughly half their sample.

In their 2007 paper, Liu et al. extended their 2002 study by using forecasts of operating cash flows, dividends, and earnings to compare the forecasting performance of earnings and cash flow multiples in several countries. They concluded that valuations based on earnings forecasts are remarkably accurate, suggesting that earnings multiples be preferred over cash flow multiples.

In discussing the various relative valuation models, Alfred Slager, from the TIAS School for Business and Society and the Dutch pension fund SPH, commented that the choice of one method over another more or less depends on the horizon, adding,

> I tend to discard [the information from market multiples] for individual stocks. Having once been a portfolio manager and tracking this information made me realize that financial analysts also suffer from a form of peer pressure—the forecast returns or multiples were too closely clustered.

The close clustering of multiples was commented on by McKinsey consultants Nolan Foushee, Koller, and Mehta (2012, pp. 1, 4). Noting that within mature industries and regardless of performance, multiples vary little among true peers, they remark,

> Companies may occasionally outperform their competitors, but industry-wide trends show a convergence of growth and returns that is so striking as to make it difficult for investors, on average, to predict which companies will do so. … Across the economy, we have found substantial convergence of revenue growth across companies.

They cite Wal-Mart and Starbucks as examples of companies whose multiples have fallen into line with those of their peers as growth slowed.

Figure 2.2, which is based on their article, shows the median portfolio growth, in percentage terms, of US nonfinancial companies grouped by comparable revenue growth at the time of portfolio construction.

Because any valuation approach has limits (e.g., the present value approach requires additional consideration of market factors; the comparables approach is less meaningful in overvalued markets), using a combination of approaches is perhaps a natural conclusion. Lleo remarked:

> To a great extent, market multiples are a reflection of current supply-and-demand conditions. This makes them valuable as a summary measure to complement a DCF approach or as a quick rule of thumb to get an initial estimate of how cheap or expensive an asset is. However, they do not scale

Figure 2.2. US Nonfinancial Companies Grouped by Comparable Revenue Growth at Time of Portfolio Formation

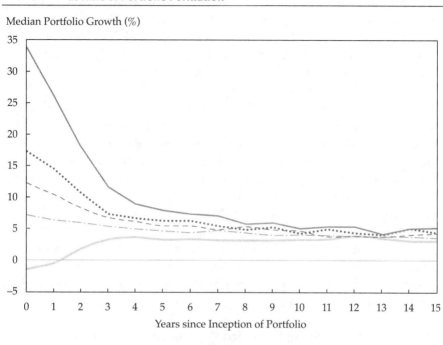

Notes: Companies were those with inflation-adjusted revenue of at least $200 million that were publicly listed from 1963 to 2000. Companies were divided into five portfolios based on their growth rate at the midpoint of each decile (1965, 1975, 1985, and 1995). Portfolios were then aligned chronologically from Year 0 to Year 15, and their median growth rates were compared. *Source:* Nolen Foushee et al. (2012).

easily (is the P/E ratio of a small firm comparable to the P/E ratio of a large firm?) and are overly sensitive to the choice of a universe of comparable firms (can we compare the EV-to-EBITDA ratio of two firms with different strategies and product mix even if they appear to compete in the same sector?).

This means that we cannot rely solely on a relative measure to value stocks. Their main use is to complement DCF methodologies by providing additional vantage points from which we can assess the value of a corporation.

Cornell and Gokhale (2016) developed a corporate valuation model that uses both market comparables and the DCF method. Their valuation model—which they call an "enhanced multiple" corporate valuation model—is based on the implied cost of equity capital. It takes into account the full term structure of earnings forecasts but does not require the estimation of the cost of equity capital. In empirical tests, they found that their model performs significantly better than the DCF model but only slightly better than standard market multiples methods; like the multiplier models, it requires the identification of comparable companies.

The use of market multipliers is associated with traditional active management but is not the exclusive preserve of traditional managers. For example, the indexing pioneer Research Affiliates does what it terms "fundamental indexing," which uses a firm's fundamental attributes, such as sales, earnings, book value, or a combination of these, in establishing index weights and rebalancing an index. Clearly, fundamental indexing is no longer a passive strategy. In the 19 October 2016 *Wall Street Journal* article "The Hidden Weaknesses of Index Funds" (see Jakab 2016), Robert Arnott, the founder of Research Affiliates, says that the firm has found that weighting an index by individual fundamental attributes such as earnings, sales, book value, or a combination of such factors is superior to weighting an index by company market capitalizations.

Additional Questions Concerning Valuation Methods

From the previous sections, one can reasonably conclude that fundamental investing, though theoretically sound in practice, requires skilled judgment. Methods based on multiples cannot be considered theoretically sound but are robust heuristics that require a considerable amount of judgment. Let's address some additional questions regarding valuation.

Can Equity Valuation Models Be Trusted?

The concept of future prospects and particularly of continued growth in the future invites the application of formulas out of higher order mathematics to establish the present value of the favored issue. But the combination of precise formulas with highly imprecise assumptions can be used to establish, or rather justify, practically any value one wishes, however high, for a really outstanding issue. (Graham 1949, pp. 315–316 in revised fourth edition)

In Penman's recent article "Valuation: The State of the Art" (2016), he focuses on valuation as business valuation and accounting:

Investing is not a game against nature, but against other investors. Thus one does not have to discover a value as if it exists in nature; the onus is not on an analyst to come up with a valuation, but merely to accept or reject the value in the market price. Accordingly, valuation models are not for valuation; they are for challenging the market price. ... But that challenge is successful only to the extent of the quality of the accounting in the valuation model. (p. 22)

Richard Bernstein, chief executive and CIO at Richard Bernstein Advisors and formerly chief investment strategist at Merrill Lynch, offered another angle: valuation models as a tug of war between buyers and sellers. Bernstein commented,

Valuation is in the eye of the beholder, and there will always be a bid–ask spread between the buyer's and the seller's valuation. There is a tug-of-war between the seller of the asset and the buyer, and how high up the income statement one values a company (i.e., sales instead of earnings) demonstrates who is winning that tug of war. As an investor, one wants to skew the analysis as much as possible in one's own favor. Yet, most valuation models are based on a "pure" valuation, which typically favors the seller.

He added that, in his experience, using GAAP earnings rather than operating earnings, EBIT, EVA, or other measures resulted in better portfolio performance.

What Drives Valuations? Even assuming that we can determine the intrinsic or at least the relative price of a firm's stock by using valuation models, a number of important questions remain. First, what drives the valuation methods? Although the idea that growth alone drives multiples is widely believed, McKinsey consultants Goedhart, Koller, and Wessels (2005) write, "In reality, growth rates and multiples don't move in lockstep. Growth increases the P/E multiple only when combined with healthy returns on invested capital, and both can vary dramatically across companies" (p. 8).

MSF Investment Management's institutional portfolio manager Robert M. Almeida, Jr. (2016) writes, "Fundamentals drive cash flow, cash flow drives profits, and profits drive stock prices" (p. 3). Citing Compustat's EPS data for the 1994–2015 period, which are shown in **Figure 2.3**, Almeida continues,

When we look back at companies that have made money versus those that haven't, we see those with profits outperforming those that lose money, which isn't surprising. But the magnitude of the performance is significant. Over the past 20 years companies that were profitable were up more than 650% (cumulative), while unprofitable ones were down 23%. (p. 2)

Robert Jarrow, professor of investment management at Cornell University, suggests that market prices are set not by fundamental values but by expected (or desired) resale values. In a recent paper on equity prices, Jarrow (2016)

Figure 2.3.   Cumulative Return for Positive and Negative Earnings, 1994–2015

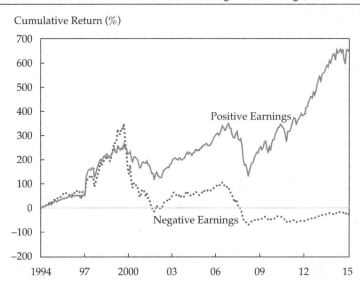

Note: Each portfolio of positive and negative earnings companies was rebalanced monthly and market cap weighted.
Sources: Almeida (2016); Compustat EPS data as of 31 December 2015.

addressed the problem of pricing "anomalies"—those based on, for example, firm size, B/M, price momentum, and seasonal effects. He suggests that asset-price bubbles are the norm, not the exception, and that most stocks have small price bubbles representing between 1% and 25% of their value. These bubbles represent the expected resale value of the shares.

The Macquarie Equities Research team (2013b) also points to the limitations of valuation models in identifying mispricings. Stocks, they say, can be driven by factors that are difficult to capture within a valuation model. Among these factors, they mention stock sentiment, management quality, earnings visibility, and leverage—as well as the need to complement mispricing signals with news flows on, for example, corporate action. (See Chapter 4 for more on mispricing signals.)

Do Valuation Methods Have Predictive Power?   The second key question is: Do valuation models have predictive value?

Brian Jacobsen, chief portfolio strategist at Wells Fargo Asset Management, with over $450 billion in assets, suggests caution in using intrinsic value to make predictions as we do not know the time period over which reversion to intrinsic value is likely to take place, nor do we know the stability of intrinsic value:

> Intrinsic value is supposed to serve as a type of gravitational pull for the market price of a stock, but too few analysts try to figure out how strong that pull is. How long will it take to have the market price converge to intrinsic value? How does the intrinsic value change as you wait? Factoring in the uncertainty around how long you might have to wait and the uncertainty around how the intrinsic value might change while you wait should make even the best of analysts more humble in the way they put client capital at risk.

Ang and Bekaert (2007) looked at the predictive power of the present value model. In their widely cited paper, they report that they did find predictability in stock returns but suggest refocusing the debate in three directions:

> First, our results suggest that predictability is mainly a short-horizon, not a long-horizon, phenomenon. Second, the strongest predictability comes from the short rate and not from yield variables with price in the denominator. ... Third, there are tantalizing cross-country predictability patterns that appear stronger than domestic predictability patterns. (p. 47)

ATP's Kjaer commented,

> In the inter-sector cross section, we do find some predictive power in relative valuation models. Obviously, stocks can be/are cheap/expensive for a reason, but on average, we still find value in these models in the cross section. Across time or sector, we have at present a relatively low conviction in these types of models. However, in the case of extreme mispricing relative to the model, we do have some confidence in these types of signals across time.

As for the widely used price-to-earnings ratio in its 10-year cyclically adjusted version (CAPE), the model was found to have little short-term predictive ability in a study by Antti Ilmanen (2016), principal of the quantitative asset management firm AQR Capital Management. Using the range of CAPE values without anticipation of information (i.e., using information that would have been known at the time the model was applied to time the market) and going back to 1900, Ilmanen found that, over the full period, the use of CAPE as a predictive model only "mildly" outperformed a buy-and-hold strategy, with all the outperformance occurring in the first half of the sample. It would have underperformed for the last 50 years of the 20th century. His conclusion: Neither a doubling of the market nor a historically high valuation is a reliable sell signal; only with hindsight is CAPE of use in the predictability of future returns and hence as a market-timing measure.

The Amsterdam-based asset manager Robeco Institutional Asset Management (2016), whose preferred approach to equity valuation is CAPE, agrees that the valuation method is not a timing factor for short-term returns, but it has found that CAPE does have some (not to be overstated) predictive power for medium- to long-term returns.

Lleo believes that relative valuation models may have some additional value as summary measures of market conditions. In particular, he remarked that Campbell and Shiller (1988) showed that the log of the P/E, calculated by using a moving average of earnings over the previous 10 years, has predictive value with respect to real S&P 500 prices over a 10-year horizon. Lleo added,

> The current relatively high value of the CAPE does not imply that returns will be lower in the future, but it suggests a significant and rising probability that the inflation-adjusted returns on the S&P 500 over the next 10 years will be low, and possibly negative. As with anything related to probabilities, the outcome is never certain. We can only look at how these probabilities are changing and adjust our investment strategy to this change.

Brandes's Little agrees. He said that the firm believes the relatively high CAPE likely portends lower future long-term returns but added that CAPE says little about near-term future returns. These returns, he said, are probably driven by sentiment and supply/demand dynamics as opposed to fundamental value:

> We believe that market prices are mean reverting to some long-term average when viewed in aggregate. While individual company returns may vary greatly, aggregate returns for the market will be more a function of factors such as real economic growth, demographics, and productivity improvements.

Bradford Cornell (2014) looked at the relationship between the dividend-to-price ratio and stock returns, internationally and over time. His objective was to determine whether the relationship is constant and, therefore, predictive of future returns. He found that although the dividend-to-price ratio has been widely reported to be effective when applied to US data, it is not necessarily predictive of future returns globally or over time. Its effectiveness varied from country to country and over time for a given country.

Can Asset Managers Take Advantage of Mispricings? The third key question is: Supposing that valuation models allow active managers to identify underpriced equities, can managers actually take advantage of such price "anomalies"? In a recent interview with Daniel Ben-Ami (2016), Burton

Malkiel, emeritus professor of economics at Princeton University and the author of *A Random Walk Down Wall Street* (1973), remarked,

> If it were true [that active management can outperform the market by identifying underpriced assets], then why is it that when you look over the last several years that it isn't two-thirds of the managers that are outperformed by the index but more like 80–90% of the managers?

What If Peer Firms or Whole Markets Are Mispriced? The fourth key question: What do investors do if the comparables are mispriced or, more specifically, when valuations of a sector or the whole market are high? Consider, for example, the telecommunications, media, and technology (TMT) sector in the period 1995–2001, when valuations were detached from economic fundamentals. Before the bubble burst, leaving investors with a loss of $5 trillion in the market value of TMT companies from their high of March 2000 to their low in October 2002, value investors saw clients walk out the door in search of higher returns. *Alpha Architect* blogger David Foulke (2016) notes that in the period of July 1998 to the end of February 2000, the NASDAQ was up 145%, while Warren Buffett's Berkshire Hathaway was down 44%, underperforming the NASDAQ by 189 percentage points. Lleo remarked,

> Overall, the return of financial assets, such as stocks, cannot stay disconnected very long from economic growth. This was Warren Buffett's central thesis when he proposed the market-value-to-GNP ratio as a measure of mispricing shortly after the dot-com bubble burst.

Do Prices Return to Some Historical Mean? Implicit in the above question is the question of a market mean—for individual assets and the market in general. With market valuations as measured by the cyclically adjusted CAPE in September 2017 some 70% above their historical average, can we assume that the relatively high valuation implies that returns will be low in the future? That is, will the CAPE return to some historical average? Or, more generally, are market valuations mean reverting to some (long-term) average? For, if there is no mean reversion, then investment strategies based on evaluating a stock's intrinsic value and the difference between that intrinsic (or fundamental) value and its market value are of little interest.

ATP's Kjaer noted that in cases of extreme mispricing on the low side, ATP analysts find that in general, "expensive P/Es" across time have relatively low prediction power. He added, "They do seem to revert but over very long time horizons, and, in addition, it is a question mark as to whether and when the mean reversion is due to the P or the E."

PGGM Investments' Lanters agrees that mean reversion is "definitely a long-term phenomenon, impossible to use for timing the market. It would be a very poor compass." His colleague Jaap van Dam, the firm's principal director of investment strategy, remarked,

> Personally, I am becoming more and more convinced that a time-varying risk premium is something in market valuation that informs long-term expected returns. If you look at CAPE, Shiller himself suggests that the more expensive decile will generate lower future expected returns versus a low CAPE, which indicates higher future returns. There is some information in this, but you must look at the circumstances.

Slager commented on mean reversion and its applicability to portfolio management, saying,

> As an aggregate indicator, I find information [obtained from the market valuation exercise] very important. Research on ALM [asset–liability management], P/E valuation, etc., suggests a simple rule of thumb: Starting valuations matter for the midterm returns, with an inverse relationship. Intuitively, this makes sense too. For example, the lower the CAPE, the higher the expected risk premium should be. In that sense, there seem to be mean-reverting elements at work.

> The problem is that in a portfolio context, there needs to be some agreement on the investment horizon during which mean reversion might materialize—7–10 years, for example—and it needs to be firmly embedded in the investment policy framework. The investment horizon of trustees and regulators (and investment managers for that matter) tends to be shorter than the horizon needed to exploit the mean-reverting opportunities. This means that the governance of the investment process should be inspired by Ulysses: Tie the investment process to the mast; do not change course under any circumstances.

In its study "The Price Is Right," Macquarie's research group (Macquarie Equities Research 2013b) adopted the Chee–Sloan–Uysal (2013) valuation-based framework to explain stock returns.[14] The main source of data for the Macquarie group was I/B/E/S for consensus analyst EPS estimates; the region covered was Europe. The group's findings—which are in line with academic research—are that company fundamentals matter more over long investment horizons. They reported that over a one-month period, valuation

---

[14]Chee et al. (2013) formalized the Graham–Dodd approach to building a valuation-based framework to explain stock returns and show that returns can be decomposed into expected returns, returns driven by unexpected cash flow news, and unexpected discount rate news.

models explained just 3% of the returns, rising to 9%, 17%, and 25%, respectively, as they increased the investment horizon to 3-, 6-, and 12-month periods. The Macquarie Equities Research group cited the study by Chee et al. (2013) showing that company fundamentals can explain about 60% of stock returns over a five-year period.

A recent blog post by Damodaran (2016) raised a number of issues relative to the use of mean reversion, widely considered a robust underpinning of many investment strategies. Damodaran remarked that, even if one believes stock returns are mean reverting, using reversion might be tricky. First, the mean will critically depend on the time period for which it is estimated. Second, estimating the time to reversion is difficult but critical from the point of view of investment strategies. In addition, structural breaks in the markets can invalidate mean reversion. Creating a test strategy to understand the ability of CAPE to predict returns, Damodaran found that CAPE is better at predicting short-horizon returns than long-term returns. Results, however, depend on the choices made in estimation: Different results can be obtained if slight changes are made in the estimation parameters. Damodaran concluded with a warning that in these times of economic change, one has to be particularly attentive in using ideas such as the mean reversion of CAPE. "Statistical significance is not cash in the bank," he wrote.

Another skeptical view on the use of mean reversion in asset management comes from Charles Schwab's Greiner:

> I personally subscribe to the concept that financial asset prices and metrics like valuation generally never mean-revert. Mean reversion implies stationary behavior in the time series. Since market prices are nonstationary, there really is no mean to revert to. In physics (and in finance), the behavior called "mean reverting" is more correctly called "anti-persistent," as in the physics of signal processing.

What about Momentum Markets in Which Asset Prices Deviate from Their Intrinsic Value? Valuation is typically considered the preserve of fundamental active managers who, with their research, keep markets efficient; trend analysis is considered the preserve of quants and index managers. Investors using pattern or trend analysis have been accused of creating momentum markets responsible for pushing stock prices up (or down) relative to their intrinsic value. Quants reply that active managers can be guilty of herd behavior that creates momentum markets.

These views were debated in 2014 by the quantitative fund manager Man AHL's academic advisory board (Man Group 2014). Nicholas Barberis, a participant in the debate and professor of finance at the Yale School of

Management,[15] argued that value investing and momentum investing might actually be more similar than they appear: "According to under-reaction theories of momentum—for example, the slow diffusion of information theory—a stock that has been trading up is also a cheap stock: not all information about it has been absorbed into the price" (p. 5).

Barberis added that "momentum traders are actually expediting the incorporation of fundamental information into prices" (Man Group 2014, p. 5), thereby helping the price-discovery process. Other participants noted that analysts' "stories" about fundamentals also play an important role in moving prices, for example, in driving up prices of TMT firms before the dot-com bubble burst in early 2000. Douglas Greening, former chief risk officer at Man AHL, asked: "What is the difference between buying really hard into a story and momentum trading?" (Man Group 2014, p. 5).

Slager had a different take on trend analysis:

> Trend analysis is an answer to our fundamental psychological need to observe patterns and make sense of the world, the stock market, because the other answer—returns and patterns are highly randomized—makes us highly insecure. Trend analysis is potentially destabilizing, but with a twist. Due to momentum effects, it tends to extrapolate downward and upward trends. However, stock markets tend to be choosy: In my observation, the upward-trend forecasts are followed when stock markets are up while, on the other hand, the upward-trend (i.e., mean-reversion) forecasts are ignored when stock markets are down. Rationally, investors should act the other way around. So, it is not so much trend analysis that is destabilizing as the selective interpretation of the investors in the market.

ATP's Kjaer observed that although anecdotal evidence in the very short term might indicate that trend analysis leads to instabilities, in the medium term, he does not consider this to be the case. This seems to be the evaluation of most persons who gave their opinion on the issue.

Lleo remarked that trend analysis and momentum investing have developed rapidly, parallel to the rapid development of statistical and machine learning adopted by trading desks, saying,

> When implemented by a single trader, a momentum strategy will seldom lead to price disruption. However, the collective action of a large number of market participants implementing similar strategies will be procyclical, leading to an increased risk of price instability and market disruption. This is especially true when these strategies are implemented via algorithmic trading without human intervention. As more algorithms identify the

---

[15]For his papers, see http://som.yale.edu/nicholas-c-barberis.

same trend, the trading activity creates a feedback loop, which may lead to an amplification and acceleration of the trend. The risk of a flash crash becomes substantial. These phenomena are particularly dangerous because they are nonlinear, which makes them difficult to predict.

Lleo suggested putting safeguards in place: "Computing an intrinsic value and using this value as an anchor in a trend-following algorithm—for example, if you are more than X% above/below the intrinsic value, then stop following the trend—can reduce the risk of following the crowd into flash bubbles and crashes."

What about Investor Objectives? A general question is, What are the objectives of the investor? Is the investor striving to beat the market or achieve some other goal? For Slager, the objective of a pension fund is not to beat the market—a chapter he considers time to close—but to help the fund achieve its goals. He cited added value for active managers in working with funds to create new metrics and strategies to aid the fund to reach its goal. "Trustees," he said, "no longer need to be drawn into overly technical asset-pricing discussions but can focus, instead, on what matters—assessing where active management can work."

3. Valuing Hard-to-Value Equities

What about valuing hard-to-value assets, such as initial public offerings (IPOs) and privately held firms? What data and tools do analysts have, and how relevant are they in the valuation process? Let's start by looking at IPOs.

Valuing IPOs

Clearly, valuing IPOs can be problematic. Warren Buffett once famously said that if he were teaching a finance course, he would ask students to evaluate an internet stock, and any student giving an answer would flunk.[16] (He made this statement at a time when no internet stock had yet made a profit.)

In May 2016, *Investopedia*'s John Burke noted that 72% of the IPOs issued in 2015 were trading below the issuance price a year later and that the average return for a 2015 IPO stock issued in the United States was –19%. According to data from FactSet, from 1 January to 23 December 2016, while the S&P 500 Index was up 10.8%, the First Trust US IPO exchange-traded fund (ETF) was up only 6.6% and the Renaissance IPO ETF was actually down 0.4% on a year-to-date basis. The problem of IPOs trading below their offer price and/or underperforming with respect to the overall market has led to a loss of investor appetite, which is reflected in the number of companies going public on US exchanges. According to FactSet analyst Andrew Birstingl (2016), only 106 IPOs were issued in 2016—the lowest number since 2009, when 64 companies went public. The amount of money collectively raised by these 106 IPOs was also down—to $20.2 billion (a 38.1% decline from 2015), the smallest annual total since 2002, when gross proceeds were $19.5 billion.

Perhaps the IPOs that most retain the media's attention are technology IPOs, where performance has not been stellar. According to Reuters reporter Dan Burns (2017), globally, shares of the 25 largest technology IPOs performed poorly in their first 12 months on the public market: 16 of the 25 suffered declines from their debut-day closing price, with 8 of the 10 biggest falling by 25%–71%. The median one-year performance of the largest technology IPOs was –22.3%. The medium-run performance of Snap's stocks following the 1 March 2017 IPO will likely affect investors' appetite for IPOs throughout the year.

Another explanation for the recent dearth of IPOs is offered by Gao, Ritter, and Zhu in "Where Have All the IPOs Gone?" (2013). They note that

---

[16]To view a related video, see www.youtube.com/watch?v=nrSB1sLgWLE.

the drop in IPO offerings was especially high among small firms and hypothesize that the advantages of selling out to a larger organization have increased relative to the benefits of operating an independent firm.

Back in 1994, Ibbotson, Sindelar, and Ritter (1994) wrote, "The market has a great deal of difficulty in valuing issuing firms appropriately" (p. 66). They identified three anomalies still present in IPO valuations today: (1) short-run underpricing resulting in first-day returns that average 10%–15%, (2) cycles in the volume of new issues and the magnitude of first-day returns, and (3) long-run (five-year) underperformance. Ibbotson et al. consider these anomalies a challenge to the efficient market hypothesis and conclude that raising capital "is subject to the whims of the market, as well as the fundamentals of the company" (p. 74).

So, what tools do analysts have for valuing IPOs? Essentially, the same tools discussed in Chapter 2 that sell-side and buy-side analysts use to value publicly traded companies, but with some additional problems.

Penman (2016) comments thus on the valuation of IPOs:

> While one cannot hope to pin down "intrinsic value" with certainty, valuation aims to reduce uncertainty in investing, and standard approaches that often introduce uncertainty do not serve us well. They even lend themselves to "playing with mirrors." Sell-side bankers like the models; set with the "due-diligence" task of supporting an issue price with a formal valuation, they look for a model that can establish, or rather justify, practically any value one wishes, however high, for a really outstanding issue. But the investor on the buy side of that issue, or a fiduciary of other people's money, is cautioned: *caveat emptor*; beware. (p. 4)

In "Valuing IPOs," Kim and Ritter (1999) consider the usefulness of various approaches as benchmarks for valuing IPOs. They report that valuing IPOs on the basis of P/E, price-to-sales (P/S), enterprise value-to-sales, and enterprise value-to-operating cash flow ratios has some predictive value when used with earnings forecasts and adjusted for differences in growth and profitability. However, the authors found that, when used with historical accounting numbers, multiples are imprecise in their ability to forecast future cash flows of IPOs. They report a similar finding for another widely used valuation method—the discounted cash flow (DCF) method.

Commenting on the use of market multiples for valuing IPO-issuing firms, An Yan, a professor of finance at Fordham University's Gabelli School of Business, said,

> The use of multiples to value listed firms where you have reliable earnings and information sources is OK, but using multiples to value IPOs is problematic: It is hard to define comparable firms, firms in an early stage of

development. An issuing firm cannot be compared to a listed firm: It might be an industry leader in a new market.

In valuing young companies with low sales volumes and negative profits, nonfinancial multiples might shed some light on valuation despite uncertainty about potential market size, profitability, and required investments. McKinsey consultants Goedhart et al. (2005) write:

> Nonfinancial multiples compare enterprise value to a nonoperating statistic, such as Web site hits, unique visitors, or the number of subscribers. Such multiples, however, should be used only when they lead to better predictions than financial multiples do. If a company can't translate visitors, page views, or subscribers into profits and cash flow, the nonfinancial metric is meaningless, and a multiple based on financial forecasts will prove a superior result. Also, like all multiples, nonfinancial multiples are only *relative* tools; they merely measure one company's valuation compared with another's. As the experience of the late 1990s showed, an entire sector can become detached from economic fundamentals when investors rely too heavily on relative-valuation methods. (p. 11)

For Ibbotson et al. (1994), the difficulty in using comparable firms' multiples (and other valuation methods) for valuing IPOs opens the door for a role for investment banks. They write, "Because using the midpoint of the offer price range results in smaller prediction errors than using comparables, investment bankers apparently are able to do superior fundamental analysis" (p. 436). The authors suggest that because of the dynamic information exchange between the investment bank and institutional investors, banks are able to achieve additional accuracy before setting the final offer price.

Peter Roosenboom (2012), professor of entrepreneurial finance and private equity at the Rotterdam School of Management, found that underwriters typically arrive at fair-value estimates by using three valuation methods—multiples, dividend discount models, and DCF models—and that all three valuation methods have similar accuracy, explainability, and (positive) bias with respect to equilibrium market value. Using reports from underwriters of their pre-IPO valuation process on 228 IPOs on the NYSE Euronext Paris for the years 1990–1999,[17] Roosenboom also found that underwriters, in an attempt to encourage investor participation, deliberately discount fair-value estimates when setting a preliminary offer price. "First-day underpricing is part of the IPO process," he commented. "It is the indirect cost of going

---

[17]Unlike US or UK law, French law makes available how underwriters value companies and the methods they use at a stage prior to taking a company public. Several other European countries have such laws.

public. Part of underpricing is due to the deliberate price discount that attracts investors in the early stage of the IPO process."

Yan discussed the two-step process in valuing and pricing IPOs. In the first step, the investment bank performs due diligence—the S-1 filings and balance sheet analysis—to arrive at a rough idea of value based on fundamentals. The second step is the "road show," during which the investment bank tests initial investor sentiment. "This," Yan noted, "is key." He continued,

> The price is determined by the industry perspective and the marketing environment. This is very important in pricing an IPO. In the end, the price is determined by the information exchange between the underwriter and investors, not so much by fundamentals. An investment bank cannot underprice an IPO on grounds of the fundamentals—which might be detrimental to the interests of the issuing firm. The underwriter must find the match between demand and the price. It is a question of market timing. Firms wanting to issue an IPO find a window to go public and do so when the market is receptive. The price depends on market sentiment, demand at the moment of going public. It is not a question of fundamental value.

The positive role of investment banks as underwriters was studied by Bajo, Chemmanur, Simonyan, and Tehranian (2016) in their paper on underwriter networks, investor attention, and IPOs. The authors studied how central lead underwriters arrive at pricing through an information exchange with their investment banking network. This information exchange allows the underwriter to both disseminate information on the issuing firms and simultaneously extract information from institutional investors that will prove useful in pricing the IPO. Bajo et al. found that IPOs underwritten by more central lead underwriters are associated with higher absolute values of offer price revisions, higher IPO and secondary market valuations, and higher IPO initial returns. The authors also found that IPOs underwritten by central lead underwriters are typically covered by a larger number of financial analysts, have large institutional investors holding shares, and (subsequently) have greater secondary market liquidity and better returns over a period of six months to one year after issuance.

Matteo Bonaventura (now a buy-side analyst at Banor SIM) and Giancarlo Giudici (2016) documented the positive role of pre-IPO book-building activity in valuing and pricing IPOs in the Italian market for the 2000–09 period.[18] Noting that one of the most common techniques used in

---

[18]As in France, Italian law makes available information about how underwriters value companies and the methods they use at a stage prior to taking a company public. *Book building* is the process underwriters use to assist in price discovery when seeking to raise equity for

valuing IPOs, according to prospectuses, is the DCF method, the authors performed reverse engineering to discover the short-term profitability implied in the offer price. Their findings revealed that although a substantially large mean forecast error was characterized by a significant optimistic bias in the estimation of the future profitability, compared with *ex post* realizations, such errors also characterize estimations by analysts evaluating non-IPO companies. They further noted that pre-IPO book-building activity plays a large role in reducing the forecast error and revising expectations, whereas forecast errors are not reduced by the market price of the first day of trading.

The significant optimistic bias in the estimation of future profitability compared with *ex post* realizations that Bonaventura and Giudici (2016) observed was studied by two academics (at that time) with degrees in engineering at the start of their academic training, Amiyatosh K. Purnanandam and Bhaskaran Swaminathan.[19] Both were at Cornell University's Johnson Graduate School of Business when they researched their paper "Are IPOs Really Underpriced?" (Purnanandam and Swaminathan 2004). They studied more than 2,000 relatively large-capitalization IPOs in the 1980–97 period. Despite the well-known phenomenon of initial underpricing, they found that at the offer price, the median IPO was significantly overvalued relative to valuations based on industry peer price multiples, such as price-to-EBITDA, P/S, and P/E. Depending on the peer-matching criteria, overvaluations ranged from 14% to 50%. Cross-sectional regressions showed that the IPOs in the study provided first-day returns but low long-run risk-adjusted returns. Purnanandam and Swaminathan write that the overvalued IPOs in their study had lower profitability, higher accruals, and higher analyst growth forecasts than "undervalued" IPOs. *Ex post*, the projected high growth of overvalued IPOs failed to materialize, while their profitability declined from pre-IPO levels. The authors suggest that investor overconfidence might be at play.

Severin Zörgiebel (2016a), a researcher in finance at Goethe University Frankfurt, studied the valuation of 2,655 US IPOs between 1994 and 2013, a period that stretches from before the dot-com bubble and its bursting through

---

clients via a public offering—either an IPO or a follow-on public offering. The bids and the number of shares that a bidder wants at the bid are collected from both institutional and retail investors during the period the offer is open. After the bidding process is closed, the issue price to be used by the underwriter is then determined by the demand generated from the book-building process.

[19]Purnanandam is now a professor of finance at the University of Michigan's Ross School of Business; Swaminathan is now a partner and the director of research at LSV Asset Management in Chicago and an adjunct professor of finance at Northwestern University's Kellogg School of Management. Swaminathan's work on valuing the Dow Jones Industrial Average won a Graham and Dodd Award of Excellence from CFA Institute.

the 2008 market crash and beyond. His study includes both technology and nontechnology companies, loss-making as well as profitable IPO issuers, and already listed firms. Loss-making IPO issuers made up roughly half of all IPOs in the United States during the period studied. Using a variety of valuation methods adopted by researchers working on similar studies and valuation methods from the mergers and acquisitions field (e.g., Rhodes-Kropf, Robinson, and Viswanathan 2005), Zörgiebel found that IPOs are, in general, valued higher than listed peer companies and that IPOs with negative earnings were valued higher than IPOs with positive earnings. **Figure 3.1** shows the discontinuity of the market-to-book (M/B) premium versus the net income margin.

Another finding is that IPOs with negative earnings provide long-term underperformance relative to both listed companies and IPOs with positive earnings.

Zörgiebel suggests that factors other than higher growth expectations might be part of this phenomenon and identifies media coverage and heterogeneous beliefs as playing a substantial role in IPO valuations.

Why are investors ready to accept high valuations for IPOs? Degeorge, Derrien, and Womack (2007) explored the role of "analyst hype" (p. 1021)

Figure 3.1. Valuations of IPOs with Negative Earnings

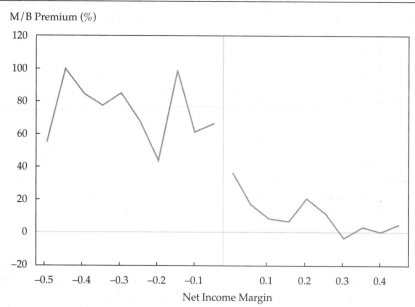

Source: Zörgiebel (2016a).

in the IPO process. In a study of the French market, they found that book building as a selling procedure was related to the perceived benefit analyst coverage provided to the success of the issuance and (possibly) post-IPO coverage in an attempt to ensure aftermarket liquidity. They also found that analysts affiliated with the lead underwriter issue more (and more favorable) recommendations for the book-built IPOs and that lead underwriters "lean on" unaffiliated analysts to provide favorable coverage. Analysts affiliated with lead underwriters were also found to put out positive recommendations ("booster shots," p. 1023) following the poor stock market performance of recent book-built IPOs.

Clearly, IPO valuations are more subject to qualitative or behavioral elements than are shares of already listed firms. Data on the fundamentals of an IPO business, such as cash flow, the balance sheet, and profitability, are often unreliable and/or not audited. Such factors as demand or the "narrative" (or marketability of the business), including assumptions about the company's future growth projections, play a large role.

Chemmanur and Yan (2017) document how advertising by firms going public affects both the valuation and price revisions of the IPO as well as long-run post-IPO stock returns. In their sample of US IPOs from 1990 to 2007, they compared IPO firms with high and low advertising intensity in the years running up to their IPOs. They found that companies going public with high advertising intensity prior to their IPOs (1) are valued higher both in the IPO and in the immediate aftermarket, (2) are associated with greater upward price revisions from the pre-IPO filing range means, and (3) have lower long-run post-IPO stock returns. Specifically, Chemmanur and Yan reported that among their sample firms, the profitability (EBIT/assets) of low-advertising-intensity firms was, on average, 9.9%, whereas that of high-advertising-intensity firms was, on average, −6.7%.[20]

Zörgiebel's (2016a) study of IPOs with negative earnings identified marketing campaigns by venture capitalists and underwriters as the valuation drivers in the IPO process. In a study specific to media coverage and startup valuations, Zörgiebel (2016b) notes that as of October 2015, Crunchbase counted 153 venture capital–funded startups in the Unicorn Club ($1 billion or over) with a (post-money) valuation of about $529 billion and total funding

---

[20]Interestingly, in their working paper "Advertising, Investor Recognition, and Stock Returns," Chemmanur and Yan (2011) found a similar pattern for listed stock returns. They tested Merton's investor recognition theory by examining the impact of advertising on stock returns and found that a higher level of advertising growth is associated with higher stock returns in the high-advertising year and lower *ex post* long-run stock returns.

of \$79 billion—about 10% of the funding of the NASDAQ 100 Index or more than 40% of the funding of the German DAX30 market capitalization.

Zörgiebel (2016b) posed the research question: What factors are driving these high valuation levels? Referring to research by Hillert, Jacobs, Müller (2014) showing that media coverage plays a large role in investor behavior in an environment of high uncertainty, Zörgiebel undertook an empirical study using Thomson VentureXpert, Crunchbase, and LexisNexis data for the 1995–2015 period. He also took into consideration technological changes, such as internet and mobile communications, that increase and speed up information exchange. His empirically based finding was that, not precluding the idea that other factors might have an incremental effect, startup (especially, Unicorn) valuations are driven to a large extent by increasing media coverage both before a venture capital–funding round and before a public IPO. **Figure 3.2** illustrates transaction value versus media coverage per day.

Figure 3.2. Average Transaction Value vs. Media Coverage per Day of 153 Venture Capital–Funded Startups in the Unicorn Club, 1995–2015

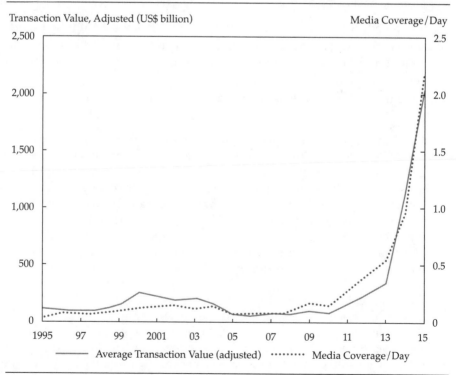

Source: Zörgiebel (2016b). Reprinted with permission.

So, is income as researched by Aggarwal, Bhagat, and Rangan (2009) negatively correlated with the offer value and the offer value positively correlated with media coverage? In general, what can be said about the long-term performance of IPOs? As mentioned, Ibbotson et al. (1994) identify three anomalies in IPO valuations, the third of which is long-run underperformance. Roosenboom remarked,

> There has been some discussion on the issue. Initial studies show poor long-term performance. A myth or a reality? It depends on how performance is measured. Are size, growth opportunities taken into consideration? What is the benchmark one is using?

> One possible reason for any long-term underperformance is offered by the theory of the divergence of opinion. According to this theory, when an IPO is first issued, optimistic investors purchase the stock, set the price. It is difficult to short-sell the stock in the early stages as the market is not yet developed. As time goes on, pessimistic sellers enter the market; short-selling begins. You then have a mix of optimistic and pessimistic buyers/sellers who co-determine the market price. It is the problem of the timing on going public.

Yan noted, "In the beginning [of the IPO process], it is hard to sell short; pessimists are not yet present in the market. Then there is profit taking over the long term. Entrepreneurs of the issuing firm exit, and there is downward pressure on the pricing."

In summing up the drivers of IPO valuations and market value, Zörgiebel said,

> Based on the general IPO literature and my research, there are many drivers of IPO valuations, the main drivers being growth expectations, profitability, ownership (venture capitalists with a good reputation, for example), underwriter quality, market timing (IPO bull phases, for example), industry/technology trends, the number of shares issued, and last but not least, the media coverage (you might call it "hype") before an IPO. It is hard to say which factors are the most important, but I guess it is often a mixture of several. In addition, these driving forces can reinforce themselves and increase or decrease valuation levels even further.

> For example, based on the theory of heterogeneous beliefs (Miller 1977), only the most optimistic investors with the highest valuations in mind participate in IPOs and receive shares. The more uncertainty there is around the value of the IPO firm, the wider the range of beliefs about the true value. As a result, extreme valuations are more likely. When the IPO firm is loss-making, has high growth expectations, and the whole situation is

fueled by media coverage and hype around that firm, uncertainty is higher, and valuation levels might be pushed upwards.

The impact of uncertainty on investor behavior was studied by Alok Kumar (2009), a professor of finance at the University of Miami School of Business Administration. Kumar found that in situations where valuation is highly uncertain and stocks are difficult to value, people are more likely to use heuristics (rules of thumb), thereby creating stronger behavioral biases and bigger investment mistakes. Kumar writes, "Both stock-level and market-wide uncertainty adversely influence [investors'] decisions" (p. 1377). These remarks pertain equally to IPOs and private equity discussed below.

The role of psychology was mentioned as a leading factor in IPO investment decision making by Sébastien Lleo, a finance professor at NEOMA Business School (France). Citing work by Hersh Shefrin suggesting that behavioral biases such as framing and conflicts of interest explain a part of the long-term underperformance of IPOs, Lleo said,

> The effect of these biases is precisely to disconnect decision makers from the type of coherent and articulated mental framework provided by DCF methods. With IPOs, as with mergers and acquisitions, the risk in the decision process of both managers and investors is that the exciting story ("writing a new page in corporate history," "grabbing some financing when the market is hot," and so on) will eclipse down-to-earth valuation. When this occurs, you may observe long-term underperformance for both the company and its stock.

Cornell and Damodaran (2014) studied the role of market sentiment in the case of Tesla Motors. Following DeLong, Shleifer, Summers, and Waldmann (1990), Cornell and Damodaran describe market sentiment as a "belief about future cash flows and investment risks not justified by facts at hand" (p. 139). Tesla went public in June 2010 (just one month after Toyota Motor Corporation announced that it was taking a 2.5% stake in the California company), with shares priced at $17. Cornell and Damodaran studied the stock's rise from $36.62 on 22 March 2013 to $253.00 on 26 February 2014. To value Tesla's shares, they constructed a DCF model and ran it at three points: before the start of the run-up in price, during the run-up, and at the end of the run-up. They found, "The valuations all yield value estimates that are well below the market price (at the time of the valuation), with the price at more than two and one-half times an aggressively optimistic value estimate," concluding that "investor sentiment played an important role in the run-up" (p. 150).

In an endnote, Cornell and Damodaran (2014) underscore the importance of the assumptions used in the models. They cite a 2014 Morgan Stanley report that put Tesla's target price at $320. That report included the DCF model used to arrive at the target price. In this case, the assumptions were a forecast of rapid growth and minimal new investment. Morgan Stanley was one of four principal underwriters of Tesla Motors' 2010 IPO. Note that at the time of writing this monograph (mid-year 2017), Tesla stock was valued at around $320.

Can the valuing and pricing of IPOs be improved upon? Banor SIM's Bonaventura remarked,

> I think that IPO prices have to accommodate the principal parties involved. Being a transaction, it is a sort of arrangement between [institutional] investors, the issuer, and the underwriters. In this case, I think that peer-group comparisons and DCF models are simply an artificial construct to justify underwriters' valuations.

Bonaventura cited recent research by Paleari, Signori, and Vismara (2014) showing that the peers selected by underwriters are systematically biased toward overvalued companies, while candidate peer firms that would make a given IPO appear overvalued are systemically excluded. The authors found that, on average, comparable firms published in official prospectuses have valuation multiples 13%–38% higher than those obtained from matching algorithms or selected by (other) sell-side analysts. They further noted that even if IPOs are priced at a discount compared with peers selected by the underwriter, they still sell at a premium when compared with alternatively selected peers. Paleari et al. suggested that this bias in an underwriter's selection of peers helps explain the poor long-run performance of the IPO.

Roosenboom's take on the possibility of improving the valuing and pricing of IPOs is as follows:

> If you look at the amount of underpricing, there is not much progress; underpricing has been steady over time and over markets. It is still the case that investors need to be enticed. Consider book building and auctions. In the United States, Google went public with an auction. The idea was that auctions led to greater efficiency in the pricing, as they provided collective information on demand. In France, for a long time, the auction process was the most prevalent, and there was less underpricing on the first day. In the auction process, you set a minimum price, and investors bid up. Through the market, it was possible to understand interest in the share, the demand. However, now the main selling mechanism just about everywhere is book building.

Fordham University's Yan agreed that the possibility of improving the valuation and pricing of IPOs is small:

Nothing can be changed. It is a question of rational investors and efficient markets. You cannot throw out theory and make a new one based on irrationality: You cannot control irrationality. Could you introduce more monitoring to the book-building process? I think we need to understand that markets will come back to rationality, efficiency. The big picture is: Markets are functioning well. Investment banks will always be rational in pricing IPOs. They have to take advantage of irrational investors. In a hot market, everyone is overoptimistic; the underwriter cannot underprice.

One possible route to improving the valuing and pricing of IPOs might be to encourage rational behavior, though our interviewees were skeptical about the possibility of changing investor behavior. Lleo said,

Individually, we have the tools to de-bias and reach more consistent values for the IPOs. But collectively, behavioral biases tend to be recurrent and resilient. I would not be surprised if we keep on observing an underperformance among IPOs for a long time.

Zörgiebel, too, suggested that creating investor awareness might help:

When investors are aware of the major driving forces and a potential bias in their thinking, they can act accordingly. Research in that area helps to detect such biases and pitfalls. Financial literacy might be the best way to improve the way IPOs are priced.

But echoing Yan's evaluation that markets will return to rationality and efficiency, he added,

There are a lot of research papers showing that investors are often far from being rational when valuing or investing in stocks—especially when there are professional and private investors active in the market with different incentives and different levels of financial literacy. Consider the so-called lottery stocks—stocks that bear high risks but also a certain amount of growth expectations. They are probably overvalued, but investors hope that these companies will turn into multi-billion-dollar companies. Some of them do—for example, Facebook. But many will fail. Investors in such stocks are not acting rationally; they are more or less gambling. It is interesting to see that IPOs are, on average, overvalued at the time of the IPO. But over time, this overvaluation decreases, and values tend towards those of industry peer groups. Apparently, the market learns over time and adjusts valuations towards the peer or intrinsic valuation. Uncertainty levels decrease, more and more hard facts about the firm become available, and valuation models can be adjusted.

Valuing Privately Held Companies

As with IPOs, many of the methodologies used in valuing privately held companies are the same as those used in valuing public companies. In particular, these methods include peer-group multiples and DCF analysis. A recent survey by the consultancy Grant Thornton ("Private Equity Valuations" 2015) found that the method most frequently used to value privately held firms is multiples (87.2%), followed by the DCF method (76.9%). In the 2015 CFA Institute Survey (Pinto et al. 2015), 92.8% of the respondents reported using multiples, and 78.8% used a discounted present value approach.

Applying these methods to evaluate privately held firms adds another set of problems to the usual challenges in using multiples or DCF analysis. Among them, Damodaran lists that (1) financial statements are likely to go back fewer years and have less detail and more holes in them and (2) debt and equity have no assigned market value.[21]

Cash flow models are the valuation method of choice for both private equity and public equity at the Dutch pension fund PGGM Investments. Jaap van Dam, the fund's principal director of investment strategy, said, "The two [public and private equity] are not so different, except that there is no liquid market for private equity—which might be an advantage." As an owner of private equity, he remarked that access to information is not a problem.

Stanley Feldman, chairman and co-founder of Axiom Valuation Solutions, which provides valuation services for private businesses, illiquid securities, and intangible assets, commented on the use of DCF and multiples for valuing private equity:

> When valuation methods used to value public firms are applied to private firms, several adjustments need to be made. First, consider the cost of capital. With few exceptions, analysts used some form of the capital asset pricing model to determine the cost of equity. Typically, a base value is estimated and a size premium is added to it. The cost of equity should also reflect a firm-specific risk premium. Although all firms have firm-specific risk, theory indicates that it may not be priced in the public markets if the marginal investor is fully diversified. In the case of private equity, the research indicates that investors in private firms are not fully diversified. This means that if the cost of capital does not include a premium for firm-specific risk, the value, all else equal, is overstated.

Feldman continued,

> Often, analysts will use an average revenue and/or EBITDA multiple for public firms to value a private firm. For example, the revenue multiple is

---

[21]See http://people.stern.nyu.edu/adamodar/pdfiles/ovhds/inv2E/PvtFirm.pdf.

determined by the net operating profit after tax (NOPAT) margin, the cost of capital (typically the firm's weighted average cost of capital or WACC), and expected growth. The multiple varies directly with the margin and growth and inversely with the cost of capital. Even if the private firm being valued has a margin and growth expectation equivalent to that of the public firm, the cost of capital for the private firm will always be higher, if for no other reason than lack of liquidity. Hence, using an unadjusted public-firm multiple to value a private firm will likely result in overvaluation of the private firm.

According to Feldman, the DCF and market multiples should be used only for mature private equity firms or private equity firms that are already in the commercial stage of development. His criticism of the use of DCF to value early-stage firms (firms that have not reached commercial development or are in the very early stages of commercial development) is as follows:

> In these cases, the analyst might use a DCF and apply a very high discount rate to reflect the firm's uncertain future, but this simply takes away the upside potential, and while this may be a low-probability event, the value achieved may be very large. So, even when multiplied by a low probability, the resulting value at the valuation date may be substantive.

Feldman believes that a Monte Carlo or option technique is preferable, though it is not generally used.

Returning to the Grant Thornton ("Private Equity Valuations" 2015) survey on methods frequently used to value privately held firms, participants cited more rule-of-thumb methods than simply DCF and multiples. These methods include the use of the price of recent transactions, such as merger and acquisition transactions (70.5%), and recent transactions involving assets that are the same or similar to the asset in question (69.2%). Feldman notes that if the transactions are private, they reflect a lack of liquidity (the methods cited above produce pre-liquidity-adjusted values). In addition, using recent transactions of comparable companies with similar attributes (e.g., industry group, recent timing, business offerings, and capital structure) is questionable, because transactions are rarely directly comparable; value might be tied to metrics other than revenue. However, in some industrial sectors where normal profitability does not vary much, there might be an industry valuation benchmark. Examples include price per subscriber in cable television or price per bed for nursing home operators.

A source of transaction data for North America is GF Data Resources' searchable database of business transactions in the mid-market ($10 million to $250 million range). Drawing from a pool of 206 private equity firms, mezzanine groups, and other financial sponsors, the firm's database has information on valuation, leverage, and specific data organized by NAICS subindustry codes.[22] GF Data Resources also provides benchmarks for meeting the Fair Value Measurement standards as mandated in the United States by Financial Accounting Standards Board Statement 157.[23] The standard calls for the use of "fair value measurement" in accounting for fiscal years and interim periods and is endorsed by, among others, CFA Institute.

In another study on methods used in valuing private equity, Gompers, Kaplan, and Mukharlyamov (2015) surveyed 79 private equity investors with a total of $750 billion in private equity assets under management as of year-end 2012. Their findings showed that despite the importance given to DCF valuation methods in academic finance programs, participants in the survey rely on internal rate of return (IRR) and multiples of invested capital (MOIC). Valuation metrics most widely used by participants were, by far, MOIC and gross IRR; the highest-ranking methods used were IRR (ranked 9.1) and the earnings multiple approach (ranked 6.1). Net present value and adjusted present value were ranked 2.8 and 0.9, respectively. A forecast horizon of five years was typical (96% of participants), at the end of which, terminal value was calculated. In discussing their conclusions, Gompers et al. write:

> The fact that [private equity firms] do not use DCF techniques is interesting. It may indicate that IRR and MOIC techniques are sufficiently robust or effective that DCF techniques are not necessary. Alternatively, it may indicate some practical deficiency with DCF techniques, especially in the private equity setting where fund structures limit investment horizons and there is considerable asymmetric information between general and limited partners. These settings may make managing via IRR-based investment decisions better. (p. 42)

Damodaran (2005) observes that the DCF model is subject to significant valuation errors if the stream of cash flows is subject to optionalities. The stock price is an option on the value of the firm. This principle, well known and applied in the model Merton (1974) proposed for valuing a firm's credit

---

[22]NAICS, the North American Industry Classification System, was developed under the auspices of the Office of Management and Budget. It was developed jointly by the US Economic Classification Policy Committee, Statistics Canada, and Mexico's Instituto Nacional de Estadistica y Geografia and was adopted in 1997 to replace the Standard Industrial Classification codes. Other classification systems exist: At the international level, Standard & Poor's and Morgan Stanley Capital International jointly developed the Global Industry Classification Standard system widely used by financial practitioners. Other systems include the International Standard Industrial Classification of All Economic Activities system developed by the United Nations.

[23]The Financial Accounting Standards Board is United States specific; the international standards are under the International Accounting Standards Board.

risk, allows a better valuation of firms when optionalities exist because of, for example, flexibility in the corporate strategy, as is typical with venture capital at seed or in the startup phase. Damodaran writes, "The equity in a firm is a residual claim, that is, equity holders lay claim to all cash flows left over after other financial claimholders (debt, preferred stock, etc.) have been satisfied," concluding that "equity can thus be viewed as a call option [on the value of] the firm, where exercising the option requires that the firm be liquidated and the face value of the debt (which corresponds to the exercise price) paid off" (p. 57). Application of real option theory is based on this observation (i.e., that the stock price is an option on the value of the firm).

Damodaran also observes, however, that applying real option theory to the valuation of firms is challenging. It requires a number of inputs that are not easy to estimate. For example, option valuation models typically make the simplifying assumption that the debt of the firm is a single zero-coupon bond. However, firms do not have only one zero-coupon bond outstanding. Estimating the volatility of the underlying value adds another layer of difficulty.

As with valuation in general, the use of more than one valuation methodology is typically recommended, because doing so allows the analyst to use one method to cross-check another. And as with IPOs, investment banks and, more generally, equity analysts play an important role in valuing privately held firms.

Summing up the valuation of private firms—an asset class estimated to be worth almost $2.5 trillion globally—staff at *Investopedia* ("Valuing" 2016) wrote that the process "is full of assumptions, best guess estimates, and industry averages." In an industry discussion organized by *Financier Worldwide Magazine* ("Q&A: Valuations" 2014), Hilco Enterprise Services' head of enterprise valuation and corporate finance, Jason Frank, said,

> Since all parties use essentially the same and well-known valuation methodologies, inputs become the most important part of the equation. If the assumptions are accurate and are properly applied within the chosen valuation methods, much of the subjectivity is eliminated and the valuation becomes more of a science. ... Regardless of which method is utilized, it is very important to scrutinise the underlying assumptions. The quality, relevancy, and accuracy of inputs separate the valuation from a "science" to an "art." A formula and its inputs can be manipulated to provide any result that is desired. A true valuation will not only follow the guideline methodologies but will be realistic in its findings.

In comparing the valuation process of private equity with that of IPOs, our interviewees noted some similarities and some differences. Lleo remarked that, as with IPOs but less consistently, the valuation gap observed with private equity and leveraged buyouts (LBOs)

> may reflect behavioral pitfalls such as overconfidence, excessive optimism, confirmation bias, and framing. When a bidding war erupts, as was the case in the 1987 LBO of RJR Nabisco, or more recently when Marriott and AnBang locked horns over Starwood, we may also observe the effect of the winner's curse.

Fordham University's Yan remarked,

> In valuing a privately held firm, fundamental values and operational efficiency are more important than they are in valuing an IPO. On the financial side of leverage, you need to be careful. If you go by sentiment, it might be hard to exit a deal. On the other hand, when you talk about the second step—that is, taking a private firm public—you encounter the same problems as in the IPO space.

As with IPOs, problems in evaluating private equity include not only the disclosure of financial information but also the importance of such factors as supply and demand. Gompers and Lerner (2000) studied 4,000 venture investments between 1987 and 1995 and found a "strong positive relation between the valuation of venture capital investments and capital inflows" (p. 283). They rejected the possibility that changes in valuation of the firms in their sample was related to the ultimate success of the firms. Specifically, Gompers and Lerner found that a doubling of inflows into venture funds led to a 7%–21% increase in the value of private equity transactions. They also found a marginal impact of a doubling in public market values, which added a 15%–35% increase in the valuation of private equity transactions.

The strong positive relationship Gompers and Lerner found between the valuation of venture capital investments and capital inflows in their 2000 study was reported by *Investopedia* journalist Ryan Downie (2016) in "Is the Private Equity Bubble Still Expanding?" Downie remarks that during the dot-com bubble of the late 1990s and 2000, global technology-sector valuations reached an average P/E 80%–300% higher than the average for equities in other sectors; for the 2010–15 period, the average P/E for public technology companies was 20—only 10% higher than the market average as a whole. Commenting on the divergence of valuation between publicly and privately held technology firms, Downie writes,

> The growth in capital earmarked for private equity was not met with a similar expansion in suitable investment opportunities. This imbalance drove valuations higher. However, publicly traded technology firms did not experience valuation expansion of the same magnitude.

The problem of valuations in public versus private markets was also the subject of an article by *Investopedia*'s Trevir Nath (2016). Writing at the beginning of 2016, Nath remarked, "The mind-boggling valuations [of private technology companies] over the past five years are more indicative of the markets than of the true value of the company itself." According to Nath, seeing private tech companies valued at 100 times revenues just before going public is not uncommon, but, he noted, apart from Facebook, almost no company has achieved a forward revenue multiple higher than 10.

Valuations appear to be high in some other sectors also. For example, in the midmarket, Pennsylvania-based GF Data Resources found that valuations for 52 completed US middle-market private equity transactions for the year 2016 averaged 6.9 times trailing 12-month adjusted EBITDA, a record high in their dataset that goes back to 2003 (see GF Data Resources 2017).

Can the industry do better in valuing private equity?

Frank remarked,

It is extremely difficult to arrive at an accurate valuation of a privately held company in today's market. Not only has the recession wreaked havoc on a business's operational, financial, and strategic initiatives, but there are many other factors that contribute to the complexity of valuing the company. Companies are faced with severe liquidity concerns, unpredictable consumer demand, and challenges to supplier relationships. These factors are creating significant uncertainty and unpredictability regarding current performance, as well as a lack of visibility for future projections, which makes accurately valuing a private entity an extremely challenging exercise.

Privately held companies are generally plagued by a lesser quality and quantity of information that can be used in an analysis. Also, a private company's capital structure could be more complex, with various classes of equity and debt securities. Lastly, the final value of a closely held, private business may differ from the value calculated using the established methods of appraisal—the income, market, and cost approaches—because various types of discounts or premiums to the basic valuation methodology must be considered. ("Q&A: Valuations" 2014)

Nevertheless, Feldman made several suggestions for improving the valuation process in private equity:

Best practice in valuation should reflect both theoretical developments in finance and economics as well as peer-reviewed research. Market practice is important, but it should conform to academic discipline where possible. Often, this is not the case. There are many examples, but one in particular relates to using public company multiples to determine perpetuity values in the DCF. There are a number of things wrong with this, but chief among them is that factors that determine the multiples at the valuation date are not likely to be the same when the firm reaches its steady state sometime in the future.

Specific to the use of DCF models, Feldman pointed to the need to test whether projections of revenue and EBIT are consistent with market expectations. This testing includes the following:

1. Making sure that changes in working and net fixed capital are at appropriate levels: Values that are too high unnecessarily burden the cash flows and reduce the value of the firm, while values that are too low do the reverse.

2. Considering depreciation a real expense: The acceleration adjustment should be added to cash flows so the full impact of the acceleration shows up in increased value.

3. Considering the perpetuity of the growth rate: This should be no greater than the expected nominal growth in the overall economy.

Feldman remarked that the same observations apply to the use of multiples, adding that public company multiples cannot be applied directly to value private firms.

Feldman also suggested the following:

1. The need to measure lack of liquidity: He suggests using a put-option pricing framework (its strength: the inputs are market metrics; its drawback: the analyst needs to determine the derivative's life).

2. The need to consider different classes of stock—preferred versus common—to reflect preferences for the latter over the former.

3. The need to make adjustments to financials, primarily the officer's compensation adjustment.

A brief look at returns on private equity investments may be worthwhile. Specific to buyout-related private equity returns, Bloomberg and asset manager Hamilton Lane Advisors analyzed private equity returns of 20 firms valued at $10 billion or more and subject to buyouts in the 2005–07 period. Their conclusion was reported by Carey and Banerjee (2016): In more than half the deals, investors would have fared better by placing their money in an index fund. A study of the performance of private equity buyout funds by L'Her, Stoyanova, Shaw, Scott, and Lai (2016) found that, using an appropriate risk-adjusted benchmark, buyout investment funds had no significant outperformance compared with a public market equivalent on a dollar-weighted basis. The authors did not, however, rule out a valuable role for buyout funds.

A decline in the industry's investment returns in the United States was documented by economists Eileen Appelbaum and Rosemary Batt (2016) at the Center for Economic and Policy Research. They reported that although details might vary, academic studies agree that private equity's performance in recent years has been about even with that of the overall stock market. This performance is in contrast to the 1990–2009 period, when the median private equity fund outperformed the S&P 500.

Nevertheless, in the low-interest-rate environment that has prevailed since the 2008 market crash, institutional investors, including pension funds—many of whose asset/liability gaps have been widening—have been increasing their allocations to private equity. Stephen Nesbitt (2016) of Cliffwater, a California-based provider of alternative advisory services to institutional investors, estimated that in fiscal 2014, private equity firms held $277 billion of US public pension fund assets—9% of the total. The result has been a significant rise in capital inflows into the asset class. According to the McKinsey Private Equity and Principal Investors Practice (2017), in 2009—just one year after the 2008 market crash—only $185 billion was newly invested in private equity globally; in 2016, the figure was $716 billion, bringing total investments in private equity to $2.46 trillion.[24]

Given the inflows into private equity, regulators and investors are increasingly focusing on valuation issues within the industry. In an attempt to protect investors, the Dodd–Frank Act in the United States and the Alternative Investment Fund Managers Directive in the European Union are looking at how asset managers' valuation policies are applied to calculate a fund's net asset value. Consistency in valuation polices is a major concern. Valuation guidelines have also been issued by the group International Private Equity and Venture Capital Valuation in an attempt to "self-regulate" the industry.

As for private equity investors, according to the endowment and foundation polls conducted by the Boston-based investment consultancy NEPC, valuation emerges regularly as investors' top concern.[25] Consider, for example, the valuation of the payment-processing specialist Square Inc. Square Inc. was valued in the private market at $6 billion in October 2014 and offered as

---

[24]In the McKinsey report, total investments in private equity at the end of 2016 were divided as follows: $1,474 billion in buyouts, $524 billion in venture capital, $315 billion in growth companies, and $151 billion in other.

[25]See NEPC's Q3 2015 and Q3 2016 survey reports and its press release about the Q3 2016 survey results (http://www.nepc.com/insights/nepcs-q3-endowments-foundations-poll-results).

an IPO on the New York Stock Exchange in November 2015 with an initial valuation of $2.9 billion—less than half its private valuation of 13 months earlier.[26] (We note that in October 2017, Square's market capitalization was $12.6 billion.) In general, according to Downie (2016), the estimate is that more than 40% of the billion-dollar technology IPOs issued between 2011 and 2015 were trading at or below their last private-round valuations as of May 2016, despite the rise in public equity indexes over much of that period.

Ernst & Young's 2015 private equity survey found that investors are asking for more detailed information about the key assumptions and inputs driving valuations. According to the survey, 69% of the participating private equity investors said transparency in financial reporting is a major concern, and 86% believe that the involvement of third-party valuation specialists adds a level of consistency to the valuation process. The following year's survey of private equity funds and investors (Ernst & Young 2016) found that for 45% of the participating investors, reporting is now the most important requirement when selecting a private equity firm; that percentage is up from 11% just one year earlier.

With investors, consultants, academics, and regulators noticing a decline in private equity returns and calling for more transparency in valuations, Feldman concluded,

> When the market for private firms is ebullient, like now, there is less time spent on ensuring that valuation methods applied are appropriate or generally consistent with best practice. Alternatively, the greater the oversight, the more likely that valuation methods applied will meet best practice guidelines. Although purchase price accounting is typically done post transaction, the analysis and methods used can inform the value of a private firm. For example, the value of the firm should line up with the value of its asset base. *Purchase price allocation* tests the veracity of a firm's value, and this is especially true when valuing a private firm. I would add that the forecast trajectory of a firm's cash flows should be subject to far greater uncertainty and that simulation techniques should be more commonly used.

---

[26]See Leena Rao and Dan Primack, "Square Prices IPO at Just $9 per Share, Valued at $2.9 Billion," *Fortune* (19 November 2015): http://fortune.com/2015/11/18/square-prices-ipo/.

4. Fair Value, Market Value, and Price Distortions

Central bank policies and corporate buybacks are the two major phenomena about which equity analysts and investors now worry because of their potential to distort market valuations relative to theoretical valuations. (Central bank policies include low interest rates and quantitative easing.) Together, these two factors are helping sustain a market rally in the United States where, for example, the S&P 500 Index has more than tripled since its March 2009 low. In Europe and Asia, where central bank policies are similar but the buyback phenomenon is (somewhat) less present, the overall picture is not dissimilar: The S&P Europe 350 Index is at about 2.5 times its 2009 low, and the Nikkei 250 Index is 2.7 times its 2009 low.

Central Bank Policies and the Market Rally

In an opinion piece published 26 October 2016, Martin Feldstein, professor of economics at Harvard University and president emeritus of the US National Bureau of Economic Research, identified the possibility of asset-price declines as one of the things that "could go wrong in America." Equity prices at nearly 70% above their historical average as measured by the cyclically adjusted price-to-earnings ratio (CAPE) for the S&P 500 in October 2016 reflected what Feldstein called "the exceptionally easy monetary policy that has prevailed for almost a decade."

At the time of this writing, most central banks continue to pursue a policy of low, even negative, interest rates. *Forbes*'s Bryan Rich (2016) mentioned Warren Buffett's evaluation of the impact of low interest rates on equity valuations when addressing *Fortune*'s Most Powerful Women Summit in October 2105. According to Rich, Buffett said that when rates are zero and expected to remain there forever, stocks would sell at 100 or 200 times earnings, because investors would have nowhere else to earn a return.[27] A decade ago, the 10-year US T-bond yield was about 4.8%; in mid-2017, after the US Federal Reserve started to raise interest rates, it was about 2.3%—close to zero or possibly negative after adjustment for inflation.

---

[27]Whether Buffett was serious is difficult to determine. A more conventional analysis would say that with a 3% equity risk premium over a riskless asset yielding zero, the stock market should sell at 33 times earnings.

Since the 2008 financial crisis, central banks have added liquidity to markets: $4.5 trillion in bond buying by the US Federal Reserve and another €1.7 trillion by the European Central Bank. In Japan, in addition to making aggressive bond purchases, the central bank has embarked on a $58-billion-a-year stock purchase program, making the Bank of Japan (BOJ) one of the country's biggest stock market investors. Kitanaka and Hasegawa (2016) estimated that by the end of 2017, the BOJ could become the largest shareholder of 55 companies in the country's Nikkei 225.

Commenting on the problem the BOJ's moves present for other investors, Kitanaka and Hasegawa cite a Goldman Sachs report:

> While the exact amount of a company's freely-traded shares is often difficult to pin down, Goldman Sachs Group Inc. estimated in an August 10 [2016] report that BOJ purchases could soak up the remaining free float at firms including Comsys Holdings Corp., Nissan Chemical Industries Ltd, and Tokyo Electron Ltd. Over the next year, if the free float in some stocks keeps shrinking, it could become more difficult for fund managers to find the shares they need to track benchmark indexes.

Note that the difficulty in tracking is a problem only if the index the manager is trying to track is not free float adjusted, but most are.

Kenneth Little, managing director of the investments group at value manager Brandes Investment Partners, said,

> We do consider many market valuations to be fairly high currently. While we are much more focused on individual companies as opposed to trying to forecast (or explain) the valuations of markets in aggregate, we do believe that record low interest rates have been a significant factor in pushing up valuation levels. The lack of alternatives for individuals and institutions seeking any sort of yield has forced investors out on the risk spectrum in order to attempt to meet their return requirements. Equities have been a primary beneficiary of this quest for yield and return, and this demand has been a key factor in driving up equity market valuations.

Matteo Bonaventura, a buy-side analyst at Banor SIM, agrees that quantitative easing (QE) and loose monetary policy have played a key role in driving equity valuations up. He noted, "Central banks have flooded the market with money. For this reason, investors needed to allocate money in the market. Given the artificial low returns of government and other bonds, equities became the target of market investors."

Jason Hsu, co-founder and vice chairman at Research Affiliates, agrees. He told *IPE Magazine* journalist Charlotte Moore (2016), "This wall of money created a spike in asset prices," with some segments of the markets becoming more and more expensive, thereby fueling a momentum market.

Alfred Slager, a professor of pension fund management at TIAS School for Business and Society at Tilburg University and a trustee at the Dutch pension fund for general practitioners SPH, gave the question quite a different twist:

> My analysis might have a slightly different starting point—and a longer horizon, a bit influenced by the work of, for example, Ulrich Beck's book *Risk Society*.[28] I think that the central banks have done impressive work in uncertain times. But the public impression is slightly different. Central banks have failed to boost the economy, while governments are struggling to hold the social fabric together of what constitutes a society or economy.
>
> These institutions are gradually being considered as low-trust organizations, while corporations are gradually being considered high-trust organizations. They have been more or less consistent in their strategy compared to governments, have their finances in order compared to governments, and are solving problems that governments cannot; consider environmental, social, and governance challenges. If this continues, it is a fundamental paradigm shift and dominates questions like valuations. So, it's perfectly possible to have today's high valuations continuing as long as the governments and public institutions do not regain that trust.

Actually, analyzing how the intervention of the central banks affects asset prices and prices more generally is challenging. The key question is why, with all the money apparently injected into the economy, little to no inflation has been seen in prices for consumer goods and services. If the growth of the aggregate measures of the money stock (as measured by M2)[29] is compared with GNP (gross national product) growth in the United States, the finding is that for the 1957–2015 period, M2 has grown more rapidly than GNP, as can be seen in **Figure 4.1**. In fact, the difference in the rates of growth of M2 and GNP accelerated as of the 1970s.

According to mainstream monetary theory, the growth of the money stock in excess of GNP growth should have some effect on the prices of goods and services. But in practice, inflation, as measured by the US Consumer

---

[28]In his book *Risk Society: Toward a New Modernity*, Ulrich Beck characterized Western societies as risk societies in which the environmental impact of production and distribution becomes increasingly central to social organization and conflict. *Risk Society* was first published in German in 1986; the first English edition was printed in 1992 by SAGE Publications, London.

[29]The US Federal Reserve defines M2 as that measure of the stock of money that consists of a broad set of financial assets held principally by households and includes bank and saving deposits, small-denomination time deposits, and balances in retail money-market mutual funds.

Figure 4.1. Growth of M2 Money Stock Compared with GNP in the United States, 1957–2015

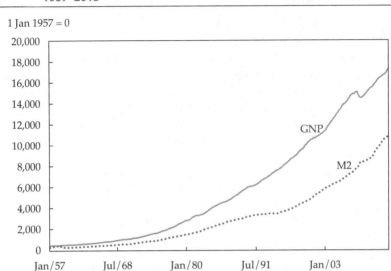

Source: Constructed by the authors using data obtained from the Federal Reserve Bank of St. Louis.

Price Index (CPI), has remained very low some seven years after the introduction of QE.

Where did the money go?

Richard Werner, director of the Centre for Banking, Finance and Sustainable Development at the University of Southampton School of Management, proposed a possible explanation. Werner (2012) argues that the newly created money did not reach the economy uniformly but that a growing fraction of the money reached financial markets, contributing to asset inflation without contributing to GDP or GNP growth or to inflation as measured by the CPI. He thus suggested the need to divide money into two streams:

- money used for GDP transactions—that is, used for the "real economy" or real circulation; "real money" (MR) and

- money used for non-GDP transactions—that is, "financial circulation"; financial money (MF).

Therefore, M = MR + MF.

Note, in particular, that QE, as it is being implemented, is by nature money that reaches primarily financial markets (MF) because QE consists of central banks buying assets from nonbank institutions. The main effect is to stimulate asset demand and therefore a rise in asset prices.

Corporate Buybacks and the Market Rally

The other important factor that market participants say is distorting prices is the dearth of shares now in public markets—in particular, in the United States.

A first explanation for the dearth of shares in the United States is due to what a study by National Bureau of Economic Research researchers (Doidge, Karolyi, and Stulz 2015) called an "abnormally" low number of listed firms in the United States today compared with the past and with other countries. The study found that the number of listed firms has declined from a high of 8,025 in 1996 to 4,101 in 2012 (the number of US-listed firms was around 4,300 at the end of 2016). According to the study's authors, delistings accounted for 46% of the listing gap; the remaining 54% is explained by the low rate of new listings. In contrast to what was happening in the United States, non-US listings increased from 30,734 to 39,427 during the same period.

A second explanation for the dearth of (US) stocks is share buybacks. Although the figure is now down slightly from recent highs, companies in the S&P 500 spent $536 billion on buybacks in 2016 (S&P 2017). Birinyi Associates estimates that US-listed firms spent about $6.1 trillion buying back their own shares during the 11-year period 2005–2016, though a drop in both authorized and executed buybacks was noted in 2016 compared with 2015.[30] The downward trend in authorizations continued into the first quarter of 2017.

Viewed from a different angle, Federal Reserve data on fund flows compiled by Goldman Sachs Asset Management and reported by Bloomberg's Lu Wang (2016b) show that US companies were the biggest buyers of stocks every year from 2009 to 2016. Indeed, in a recent *Dr. Ed's Blog* post, Edward Yardeni (2017) remarked that since the start of the bull market during the first quarter of 2009 through the end of 2016, buybacks totaled $3.4 trillion; dividends added up to $2.4 trillion. "Combined," he noted, "they pumped $5.7 trillion into the bull market, driving stock prices higher without much, if any, help from households, mutual funds, institutional investors, or foreign investors. ... The bull has been on steroids from share buybacks by corporate managers."

Share buybacks are frequent in the United States but also take place elsewhere. Using Bloomberg data, journalist Sofia Horta E. Costa (2016) reported

---

[30]We thank Birinyi's Chris Costelleo for providing us with this information in an Excel spreadsheet.

that 5 million shares were bought back by STOXX Europe 600 firms in 2015 (this number compares with more than 60 million shares bought back by S&P 500 companies in the same period). In Japan, the phenomenon has been growing in importance since 2014, which witnessed a spike in buybacks. Indeed, in 2016 corporate buybacks were the biggest source of equity demand in Japan, according to Leo Lewis (2016). Lewis cited Goldman Sachs estimates that put buybacks for the fiscal year ending 31 March 2017 at a record ¥6.5 trillion (approximately $60 billion). Nevertheless, buybacks in Japan, compared with those in the United States, still represent a small proportion of market capitalization.

An example of the effect of corporate buybacks on stock prices comes from the *Nikkei Asian Review* ("Fewer Japanese Companies" 2017). In January 2017, when NTT DOCOMO reported nine-month results without renewing its share repurchasing program, its stock price fell by 4% within a few days. In contrast, companies that announce share buybacks see the price of their shares increase. When Asahi Glass Company announced buybacks of up to ¥10 billion several months later, the company's shares went up some 9% to a six-year high. After Aoyama Trading Company announced its sixth straight year of buybacks, shares went up 3%.

Indeed, some equity analysts consider corporate buybacks the sole factor driving demand for equities in today's market. In March 2016, Bloomberg TV reported that if the pace of withdrawals from US mutual funds and exchange-traded funds were to continue through the month, outflows would hit $60 billion (Wang 2016a). The result would be the biggest annual gap between outflows and corporate buybacks ($225 billion) since the "mini" stock market crash of 27 October 1997. At the Amsterdam-based Robeco Institutional Asset Management (2016), buybacks are considered largely responsible for the growth in market multiples seen in recent years.

Buybacks, which in theory are a way of sharing profits with shareholders, increase demand for and reduce the supply of a company's shares. Given the law of supply and demand, buybacks tend to distort valuations in the immediate term by raising earnings per share (EPS), even when total net income is flat. Interestingly, for fear of market manipulation, companies were largely prohibited from buying their own shares until 1982, when the Ronald Reagan administration began to deregulate financial markets.

In a special Reuters report on buybacks, Brettell, Gaffen, and Rohde (2015a) cited the effect of the health insurer Humana's $500 million share repurchase in November 2014, which allowed the firm to surpass its $7.50 EPS target by a penny. Commenting on such buybacks, Heitor Almeida, professor of finance at the College of Business at the University of Illinois in Urbana-Champaign, cautioned against using EPS as a performance metric. "It's too easy to manipulate," he told Reuters reporters (Brettell, Gaffen, and Rohde 2015b). James Montier, a member of the asset allocation team at GMO in London, remarked that the concentration on buybacks has as its objective raising EPS, which he attributed to the objective of hitting share option targets (Brettell et al. 2015b).

As mentioned in Chapter 3, Straehl and Ibbotson (2015) concluded that the shift in corporate payout policy from dividends to buybacks has caused a "secular decrease in dividend yields, and an analogous increase in per-share growth," leading to a "structural break in the return components of the traditional supply models such as the dividend discount model" (p. 25). Chapter 3 provides the authors' proposed supply model of stock returns, which they dubbed the "total (dividends plus buybacks) payout model."

Most value managers focus on individual companies, rather than trying to forecast (or explain) the valuations of markets in aggregate, but at the level of asset allocation, investors and their asset managers have an interest in understanding the relative valuation of the investable universe. Writing back in 1996, four years before the dot-com bubble burst, University of California, Berkeley, economist J. Bradford DeLong remarked,

> The stakes for investors are truly enormous. If the $7 trillion US stock market is overvalued by a third, some $2 trillion plus of the wealth Americans now hold in stocks will vanish over the next decade as stock prices return to fundamentals. The losers will be those who remain fully invested in the market over the next decade. If stocks are not overvalued today, the losers will be those who—out of fear of possible overvaluation—spend the next decade out of the stock market, with their wealth invested in lower-return investments in bonds and in the money market.

DeLong added,

> One standard measure of "fundamentals" is average earnings over the past 10 years—an average taken over a time period long enough to smooth out business cycle fluctuations in profitability. In a typical year, a typical stock is priced at about fifteen times its 10-year average of earnings. Today the typical stock sells for nearly *thirty* times its 10-year average of earnings. ... The argument that the stock market is overvalued—and that it will come back to earth over the next decade, perhaps in a gradual deflation of prices like a slowly-leaking balloon and perhaps in a crash—is simple. Stocks are tradable pieces of paper that carry "ownership" of the earnings of American corporations. Stock price "fundamentals" are thus roughly proportional to the earnings of American corporations. But today the stock market is selling for roughly twice its typical earnings multiple.

Are today's stock markets—in the United States, the S&P 500 is now roughly 70% above the historical earnings multiple—overvalued? And if so, is the overvaluation the result (at least in part) of central bank policies and buybacks?

PGGM Investments' head of equities Felix Lanters said, "While I don't like to use the term 'overvalued,' there is a gap between market values and valuation in the models. We are having more and more trouble finding companies that are undervalued; their numbers are fading away."

Bradford Cornell, a professor of financial economics at the California Institute of Technology, agrees that prices are high but commented, "I do note that they have been this high or higher in the past when the factors to which you refer [central banks' policies and stock buybacks] were not present."

Niels C. Jensen, partner and chief investment officer at the United Kingdom–based Absolute Return Partners, identified two additional factors to explain market values—in particular, US market values. To low rates and corporate buybacks, Jensen (2015) added (1) the all-time high of capital, which is now 42%–43% of US national income, against a historical average of 35% and (2) demographics—the biggest equity buyers are middle-aged, and the US great equity bull market has coincided with Baby Boomers' middle years. Jensen contrasted the situation in the United States with that in Japan (see **Table 4.1**).

Christian Kjaer, head of global equities and volatility at the Danish fund ATP, believes that the supply–demand balance is at work. He remarked, "Supply and demand has caused 'risk-free' yields as well as risk premiums in

Table 4.1. Comparison of the Ratio of Total Market Capitalization to Gross Domestic Product for Four Major Economies and Aggregate OECD Countries

Region/Country	1975–1985 % Range	Peak, 1999–2000	2015
Germany	11–24%	65%	51%
Japan	3–36%	98%	112%
United Kingdom	24–72%	179%	120%[a]
United States	37–53%	153%	139%
OECD members	24–49%	122%	102%

[a]The data for this ratio are not available from the World Bank but come from Siblis Research (http://siblisresearch.com/data/market-cap-to-gdp-ratios/).

Note: OECD = Organisation for Economic Co-Operation and Development.

Source: Constructed by the authors using data obtained from the World Bank (http://data.world-bank.org/indicator/CM.MKT.LCAP.GD.ZS?locations=OE-DE-JP-US-GB).

general to compress. As a consequence, valuations are high not only in equities but across asset classes."

Sébastien Lleo, associate professor of finance at NEOMA Business School (France), elaborated on the interconnected factors at play in today's high valuations and asked whether they are justified by long-term trends:

> To start with, interest rates are indeed exceptionally low. This reflects the extraordinary measures that the world's leading central banks implemented in the wake of the 2007–2009 global financial crisis, but also the low inflation environment that has prevailed since the early 2000s.

He continued,

> The direct impact on valuation is that discount rates will be low, which justifies higher present values of future cash flows. At the same time, low interest rates have made money market and fixed income much less attractive, pushing cash into riskier assets and, in particular, stocks. This excess demand, at a time when the net offer of shares is muted or negative, has compressed the equity risk premium, leading again to lower discount rates and higher valuations.

> Behavioral factors, in particular the spectacular recovery of the financial markets following the global financial crisis, also play a role in shaping our expectations about the future, both in terms of cash flows and discount rates. If valuations are high, the key question we need to ask is whether these valuations are justified by a long-term trend in both cash flows and discount rates or represent an excessively optimistic and psychologically biased view of future possibilities.

A different view comes from James Montier and Philip Pilkington (2016) of GMO's asset allocation team in London. In an attempt to understand why their forecasts of S&P 500 returns had been too pessimistic over the past two decades, they found that the market's high P/E was not due to low interest rates. They asked what, then, might account for the high valuations. Studying data for the 1964–2016 period, they found that since 1984, "significant amounts of annual stock market returns … were made on FOMC [Federal Open Market Committee] meeting days" (p. 1).[31] In addition, they found that "these pre-FOMC returns have increased over time and account for sizeable fractions of total annual realized stock returns" (p. 2). Note that their research resulted in the development of what they call the Monetary-Policy-Adjusted CAPE.

---

[31]In the United States, the Federal Reserve controls monetary policy using three tools: open market operations, setting the discount rate, and setting reserve requirements. The first of these, open market operations, is the responsibility of the FOMC.

In a recent quarterly letter, Jeremy Grantham (2017), their colleague in the United States and the co-founder of GMO, observed that the P/E of S&P 500 firms is now 65%–70% higher than during the 1935–1995 period. Grantham also noted that the margins of S&P 500 firms have risen by about 30% over their pre-1997 margins. He then analyzed the sources of the increase in corporate profits and listed among them (1) the increased value of brands due to globalization; (2) increased corporate power over the past 40 years; (3) increased corporate wealth, which has been used to influence policy; (4) a decrease in capital spending as a percentage of GDP; (5) increased monopoly power for US corporations; and (6) lower interest rates since 1997, together with higher leverage. Grantham argues that these changes, as well as low interest rates, are here to stay for a long period. He warns investors,

> If you are expecting a quick or explosive market decline in the S&P 500 that will return us to pre-1997 ratios (perhaps because that is the kind of thing that happened in the past), then you should at least be prepared to be frustrated for some considerable further time, until you can feel the process of the real interest rate structure moving back up toward its old level. (p. 15)

Note that higher profitability per se does not explain a higher P/E. Higher margins and a shrinking number of new investments coupled with an increased money supply, however, have attracted an excess flow of money into the same stocks. This excess flow produces an increase in the price per unit of profit—that is, a higher P/E.

How Do We Evaluate Whether Markets in Aggregate Are Correctly Valued in Relation to Our Theoretical Values? Several market measures based on historical comparisons are typically used to judge over- or undervaluation. Among the most cited methods is the CAPE (or P/E 10), which uses 10 years of earnings data instead of a single year and adjusts the historical earnings for inflation. The intuition behind this measure is that the return to financial assets such as stocks cannot stay disconnected very long from earnings growth.

In mid-2017, the S&P 500 CAPE was around 29; the historical mean (i.e., since the 1870s) is about 16.7. In the same period, the FTSE 100 CAPE was at 15, compared to its historical mean of 16, and the FTSE 250 at 25, compared to its historical mean of about 20. Also in mid-2017, the Nikkei 225, at 28, was not far from its historical mean of 26.

Another frequently used measure based on P/E is the forward price-to-earnings ratio (price divided by next year's forecast earnings).[32] According to

---

[32]The forward P/E is calculated by taking into consideration analysts' future projections for S&P 500 earnings and the current price of the index.

FactSet analyst John Butters (2017), in mid-2017 the S&P 500's 12-month forward price-to-earnings ratio was 17.6, its highest level in 13 years.

In addition to forward-looking P/E and backward-looking measures (the trailing 12-month P/E is widely used in the industry on single assets), other measures frequently used to understand whether markets, overall, are cheap or dear include the historical growth of capital market earnings and the growth of per capita GDP, or a country's stock market capitalization as a percentage of its GDP.

Straehl and Ibbotson (2015) essentially confirmed earlier findings by Ibbotson and Chen (2003) that US long-run stock returns "participate" in the real economy. Ibbotson and Chen decomposed 1926–2000 historical equity returns using factors commonly thought to describe the aggregate equity market and overall economic productivity (i.e., inflation, EPS, dividends per share, price per earnings, the dividend payout ratio, book value per share, return on equity, and per capita GDP) and found that for the 1926–2000 period, the majority of historical returns can be attributed to the supply of these components. Straehl and Ibbotson (2015) extended the period to 1871–2014—a 143-year period—and found that total payout (dividends and buybacks) per share and per capita GDP grew approximately at the same rate, albeit with large fluctuations from time to time (p. 20).

Cornell (2010) explored the link between equity returns and economic growth in a study that took into account both theoretical models and empirical results from growth theory. He postulates that

unless corporate profits rise as a percentage of GDP, which cannot continue indefinitely, earnings growth is constrained by GDP growth. This dynamic means that the same factors that determine the rate of economic growth also place bounds on earnings growth and, thereby, the performance of equity investments. (p. 54; italics added)

Cornell concluded that the long-run performance of equity investments is indeed fundamentally linked to growth in earnings, which in turn depends on growth in real GDP.

The positive relationship between the growth of total payout per share and GDP growth found by Straehl and Ibbotson (2015) and others contrasts with the findings of Jay R. Ritter at the University of Florida's Warrington College of Business. In his cross-country study using data from the World Development Indicators for the 1900–2002 period, Ritter (2005) found a negative relationship between real stock returns and per capita GDP.

Following these and other studies, researchers at Barra/MSCI (2010) asked whether investors, assuming a relationship (or not) between economic growth and stock returns, should assign a higher weight to countries experiencing strong GDP growth. They note,

> This question is not new; "supply-side" models have been developed to explain and forecast market returns based on macroeconomic performance. These models are based on the theory that equity returns have their roots in the productivity of the underlying real economy and long-term returns cannot exceed or fall short of the growth rate of the underlying economy. (p. 1)

Using long-term Morgan Stanley Capital International equity index data (i.e., the MSCI All Country World Index and the MSCI World Index, both of which pertain only to large-cap and mid-cap companies) and the GDP growth of countries included in the same indexes, the researchers empirically tested the link between economic growth and subsequent stock returns. They observed, "Long-term trends in the link between real GDP and equity prices are more similar for global equities than for most individual [country] markets" (Barra/MSCI 2010, p. 5). In other words, the link is stronger between variations in global GDP and the return of the global index across time than it is for variations from one country to another. They offered several explanations for this finding: (1) given economic integration, the link appears over global, not national, markets; (2) a large part of economic growth comes from new, not existing, companies, which dilutes GDP growth before it reaches shareholders; and (3) expected economic growth might already be factored into share prices, thereby reducing future realized returns.

O'Neill, Stupnytska, and Wrisdale (2011) at Goldman Sachs Asset Management found significant methodological issues in previous studies that failed to establish a link between GDP and returns (e.g., problems with data, too long a time horizon, during which many changes occur) and posed a question: "Why, in a world of forward-looking investors, [would we] expect to find a contemporaneous relationship between growth and returns? In fact, there exists extensive evidence that equity price changes tend to lead GDP growth in a number of countries" (p. 3). They believe that an existing (though not straightforward) link between GDP and equity returns places a renewed emphasis on valuation. Indeed, establishing such a link lends support to present value models.

Finally, London Business School's Dimson, Marsh, and Staunton (2014) revisited this question: If a link between per capita GDP and equity returns exists, why has making money by buying stocks of countries that are improving their economic position been so difficult? For example, looking at 21 countries for the 1972–2013 period and assuming that investors put their money in the equity markets of the fastest-growing countries, the approach would have delivered an annual return of 14.5%; had the investors put their money in the slowest growing countries, they would have realized an annual return of 24.6%. The authors concluded, however, that although capturing returns is not easy, stronger (aggregate) GDP growth is "generally good for investors" (p. 29).

Another measure used to understand whether markets in the aggregate are overvalued is the ratio between a country's total market capitalization (TMC) and its GDP (the TMC-to-GDP ratio). This ratio is often referred to as the Buffett ratio because following the dot-com bubble of the late 1990s, Warren Buffett embraced the ratio of the Wilshire 5000 Full Cap Price Index to US GDP as "probably the best single measure of where valuations stand at any given moment" (Loomis 2001). As of mid-2017, this ratio for US markets stands at just above 130%. According to data from the World Bank, during the 1975–85 period, the average for the United States was under 50%, and at the end of the dot-com bubble in early 2000, it had reached a peak of 153%. Among developed countries, the TMC-to-GDP ratio has historically been highest in the United Kingdom and the United States. Table 4.1 provides a comparison of the TMC-to-GDP ratio for major economies and aggregate OECD member states for the 40-year period 1975–2015.

In referring to lessons to draw from the TMC-to-GDP ratio following the dot-com stock crash, Buffett told *Fortune* journalist Carol Loomis (2001), "For me, the message … is this: If the percentage relationship falls to the 70% or 80% area, buying stocks is likely to work very well for you. If the ratio approaches 200%—as it did in 1999 and a part of 2000—you are playing with fire." The long-term average for the United States is 79%.

The intuition behind Buffett's advice is that the stock of capital and the actual economic output should move together. Actually, the question is complex. Economies are not homogeneous. An economy's growth rate is a simplification that does not take into account the inequalities inside the economy. Different sectors in the same economy might grow at different rates for prolonged periods. But as with the relationship between the growth of total returns and the growth of per capita GDP, many value managers do not use the TMC-to-GDP ratio.

Edward Yardeni of Yardeni Research has criticized the ratio for several reasons, among them the fact that the TMC-to-GDP ratio does not take into account structural changes in profit margins caused by, for example, changing tax rates, lower interest rates, or technological innovation (Siblis Research, n.d.). It also does not take into account institutional differences between countries; for example, a great deal of the equity in German companies is family owned and thus not listed on exchanges. But again, the critical fact is that economies are complex systems with complex output. To average growth over a whole market and a whole economy is basically impossible.

5. New Tools for Equity Valuation

"It's now an era in which analysts capable of analyzing will need to do so thoroughly." These are the words of Shinichi Tamura, a Tokyo-based strategist at Matsui Securities Company, as reported by Allan and Ito (2016). But what is meant by "thoroughly" in an era of big data and high-performance computing, advanced analytics, predictive reasoning, machine learning/artificial intelligence, natural-language processing, fast algorithms, and automation?

During the past decade or two, many business processes in the financial services sector have been radically changed or fully automated. Consider algorithmic (or automated) trading. In the European Union and the United States, automated trades are estimated to constitute 50%–80% of all equity trades, up from about 33% in 2006. As for investment management, some automation has already taken place. Anthony Ledford, chief scientist at the London-based quantitative investment manager Man AHL, remarked,

> The balance sheets of publicly traded companies are reported on a timetable that is known well in advance, and they largely comprise structured summary information in a standardized format. This makes it relatively straightforward to monitor the balance sheet changes of any particular company through time. Modern production systems for data capture, storage, and retrieval can easily scale this process across the tens of thousands of publicly traded companies found in global portfolios. This is not machine learning, nor is it big data—it's simply automation.

Much progress has been made recently in data management thanks to the structuring or standardization of data brought about by adoption of the eXtensible Business Reporting Language (XBRL) required by regulators for financial reporting purposes. XBRL uses a taxonomy or list of fields that allows one to "tag" data. Tagged data are generally referred to as metadata. The objective of XBRL is to deliver financial data from companies directly in a computer-readable format, thereby making financial statements and data easy to search and comparable over time and among companies. In their study on data and technology in the financial services industry, Singh and Peters (2016) note among the benefits brought about by the implementation of XBRL the availability of more (and more granular) data. They cite more than 51 million discrete facts tagged with XBRL in the US SEC's EDGAR database of more than 89,000 filings by some 10,000 firms.[33]

---

[33]EDGAR stands for Electronic Data Gathering, Analysis, and Retrieval system.

An example of what can be done with metadata combined with artificial intelligence (AI) comes from the software firm Yseop. Its natural-language-generation software relies on metadata to generate business descriptions automatically. The financial data company FactSet runs Yseop software across its 15 highly connected and structured databases to generate hundreds of thousands of company descriptions daily. Other firms offering software to monitor data sources in real time, detect signals, and generate analyst reports include the Cambridge, Massachusetts–based AI firm Kensho and the content-summarization company Agolo.

The expectation among active managers is that the vast amounts of data, including unstructured data now available on the web, can be put to use to outperform markets. Sébastien Lleo, a professor of finance at NEOMA Business School (France), commented, "One of the important objectives of data analysis and statistics is to be able to transform raw data into information, information into knowledge, and knowledge into insights that can be used for decision making. Big data fits in this general pattern."

Among the data that active managers are anxious to use are real-time macro and micro data, such as sales and price data from points of sale, news streams, and social network data. Commenting on these and similar data sources, Gurvinder Brar, global head of quantitative research at Macquarie Equities Research, said, "Depending upon the sophistication of the asset manager, I would say that these data points are already being used, and their importance will grow over the coming years."

Peter Hafez, the chief data scientist with big-data analytics supplier RavenPack, agrees. He remarked,

> Over time, the use of alternative data sources will span the entire industry, though not all investors will adopt the new type of data. It is already being used by the most sophisticated quantitative hedge funds and asset managers, a process begun around the early 2000s. In recent years, interest for alternative data has exploded, and in the coming years, we will see more and more traditional asset managers make significant investments to become data ready. This will require an investment not only in IT [information technology] but also in data science and quantitative research. Some firms will build up internal capabilities in alternative data; others will look to buy ready-made alternative data factors or indicators that can be integrated directly into their investment process.

Axel Pierron, co-founder and co-managing director of the financial consultancy firm Opimas, noted that data sourcing and factor data are now crucial in asset management, saying,

What is new today is that with artificial intelligence, firms are trying to bridge the gap between real-time information and information with longer periodicity. The early 2000s saw the implementation of strategies and algorithms for trading, which were all similar as all were based on using market data. With the AI tools now available, firms are looking beyond traditional market data, which everyone is using, trying to build (trading) strategies with subcorrelations. As firms use a greater variety of data sources, we have seen a greater differentiation, a greater diversification of strategies.

These differences, Pierron remarked, "reduce herd behavior and lead to greater market stability." Opimas has recently published reports on the use of AI (Pierron 2017) and alternative data (Marenzi 2017) in asset management.

Much of this new big data is commercially available, however, which will eventually reduce its value. PanAgora president and chief executive Eric H. Sorensen commented,

> First, "big" alone is not a sufficient condition for added value—"big" but not "smart" (or causal) is potentially spurious. Second, "big" brings perverse results if everyone uses it. Smart data may be sufficient. Smart data, among other things, is not commercially ubiquitous, is given to reasonable investment horizons, and is rich in fundamental intuition.

Sorensen referenced his recent investment insight note (2017) relating PanAgora's first encounter with smart data back in the early 1970s:

> A major industry of the Pacific Northwest was forest products—Weyerhaeuser and Georgia-Pacific, to name a few. One innovative analyst determined that during periods of rising interest rates (building slump) versus falling rates (building boom), a small (versus large) lumber inventory separated the winners from the losers. Consequently, he hired a helicopter pilot to routinely fly him directly over the lumber yards adjacent to lumber mills, as well as active logging sites, to assess the potential inventory levels. The *helicopter data* was proprietary and intuitively causal. Most importantly, it worked, providing valuable company insights.

Sorensen continued,

> Forty-five years later the contemporary version of helicopter data is satellite imaging of shoppers' parked cars. Today's modern space technology version is big, and it seems causal. However, it may fail if everyone has access to it. Ubiquitous is neither proprietary nor innovative, which means it fails to be "smart." (p. 3)

To illustrate this fact, Sorensen cited an experiment by his colleagues at PanAgora on parking lot data for the 2010–13 period. The back test produced a 30% cumulative long–short return. But after 2013, the return became negative and remained so thereafter: In 2013, a vendor started selling the data to subscribers.

Just what data will prove useful and what analytical methods will be required to help investment professionals improve their ability to predict the value of a firm's stock? In "Finding Big Alpha in Big Data," members of BlackRock's Scientific Active Equity Group (Savi, MacCartney, Betts, and Shen 2015) identify what they consider of interest—namely, all data, and in particular, data that relate to economic human behavior. Just in the area of brokerage reports, they cite an average of 4,000 reports daily, totaling 36,000 pages—in 53 languages. They argue that because most of the data of interest are unstructured, new tools and more powerful computing platforms will be required. Among the tools they list are machine learning, natural-language processing, scientific data visualization, and distributed computing.

Another list of new tools for investment professionals was proposed by the Boston Consulting Group (Sheridan, Beardsley, Ouimet, and Baltassis 2016), whose list—somewhat expanded—includes the following:

> machine-learning platforms that can mine huge quantities of structured and unstructured data; predictive-reasoning and artificial-intelligence platforms that can reveal important portfolio effects; rapid statistical analyses that generate event studies and correlation analyses on a massive scale; semantic analyses capable of discerning context and drawing insights from various data types; visualization tools that create intuitive displays of information that would be too diverse and complex to summarize in writing; and natural-language processing engines and data aggregation platforms that give managers convenient, timely access to different forms of data.

> Armed with these advanced techniques, digitally forward asset managers can gain a significant information advantage over peers who rely mainly on traditional data sources and analytical practices. They can crunch through vast quantities of data; scour video and satellite imagery to gauge a retailer's Black Friday prospects; extract insights from social media, texts, and e-mail to divine market sentiment; and parse a CEO's comments during an earnings call to estimate the potential impact on the next quarter's results. They can discern how unexpected weather disruptions might affect their portfolio, and even disprove long-held beliefs about how markets work.

Macquarie's Brar remarked,

> These methodologies and tools are being used by quantitative managers, but to a lesser extent by fundamental investors. I do, however, see a greater desire from fundamental analysts to apply these tools within big-data space, to tease out signals which fundamentally alter their views on a single stock.

Lleo agreed:

To some extent, finance is ready for a data-centric evolution. Data—whether financial statements, economic releases, or market prices and yields—are already at the heart of finance. Market data, in particular, fit the "high-volume, high-velocity" bill, and economic data are getting ready for an upgrade, thanks to a growing interest in *nowcasting*.[34] Since the 1970s, banks have been constantly upgrading their computing power to run ever more demanding pricing and risk management algorithms.

Lleo added,

Most of this evolution has taken place in trading rooms, where the emphasis was placed on objective pricing (as in Black–Scholes-style derivative pricing) rather than subjective valuation (as in DCF [discounted cash flow]-style equity valuation). The mathematical tools and algorithms are different, because the objective is different: Pricing is about hedging; valuation is about predicting. Only recently have banks started to focus on predictions on a large scale—to predict the default risk of their individual clients. Now, machine learning–based techniques are being used in investment management to design smart-beta strategies, as well as "robo-advisers." We can well envision that machine learning will soon be used in the valuation process as well, to help analysts and portfolio managers process higher velocity data and higher variety data—including news coverage, CEO interviews, tweets, supplier and client data, supply chain information, etc.—or to explore the industries from a network perspective.

Data, Tools, and Their Application

Let's take a look at some of the methodologies and technologies at the heart of the change. First, machine learning.

Machine learning (computer programs that learn when exposed to new data) is a hybrid discipline that borrows from a range of areas, including computer science, engineering/signal processing, mathematics, and statistics. In an explanatory video, Man AHL's Ledford (n.d.) describes machine learning as

the use of algorithms for identifying and acting on repeatable patterns in observed data. It provides a suite of data-driven tools for quantifying

---

[34]*Nowcasting*, a contraction of now and forecasting, is the prediction of the present, the near future, and the very recent past in economics or the creation of accurate forecasts of undisclosed target values based on publicly observable proxy values. The term has been used for a long time in meteorology. It has recently become popular in economics, because standard measures used to assess the state of an economy (e.g., GDP) are determined only after a long delay and are subject to subsequent revisions. Nowcasting models have been applied in central banks, and the technique is used routinely to monitor the state of the economy in real time.

knowledge from ensembles of such unstructured and structured data sources, embedding their combined information within a coherent model that—importantly—does not require the modeler to make simplistic or artificial assumptions, such as linearity. The algorithms are not told what to look for but seek out the patterns for themselves, a difference with respect to other areas of data mining.

Ledford notes the approximately 1.5 billion data ticks that Man AHL receives daily in numbers and text and from other sources of information to underline the greater signaling power of machine learning over the human brain. The firm has been using machine learning–based systems in its multi-strategy client portfolios since early 2014.

RavenPack's Hafez remarked that the greater emphasis on machine learning and AI is due to the explosion of potential alpha sources or factors that require new modeling techniques that researchers are combining with traditional econometric modeling.

The quantitative research teams at Macquarie Equities Research (2015) apply textual analysis (also called "text mining" or "natural-language processing") to the transcripts of earnings conference calls for global companies. Their objective is to obtain a quantitative measure of sentiment or tone—that is, bullish or bearish—and to use that "soft information" to predict future stock returns. For the analysis, they use FactSet data and FactSet's API on the global universe of equities, coded in standard R packages, and apply the naive Bayes classifier.[35] They prefer the naive Bayes classifier because it is computationally inexpensive compared with other classification methods such as support vector machines or neural networks. The latter require expensive training of parameters.

Interestingly, their results show that sentiment does predict returns—and not only in the first few days after a conference call but also over horizons of one to three months or more. Researchers at Macquarie suggest that among the uses for the signals gained from the textual analysis of thousands of conference calls, fundamental analysts can use the signals as a screening variable to identify those corporate voices with a bullish or bearish tone or those that display a marked difference between the direction of the surprise and tone.

Commenting on Macquarie's work on text analysis, Brar said, "We've done extensive work on analyzing corporate communications—earnings

---

[35]*R packages* are collections of functions, data, and compiled code in a well-defined format. More than 4,500 packages are available. A Bayesian classifier is a statistical technique for predicting class membership probabilities. It can be used to estimate the probability that a given data point is a member of a particular class. See https://monkeylearn.com/blog/practical-explanation-naive-bayes-classifier/.

transcripts, conference call transcripts—and find these to be a good source of alpha for both quantitative and fundamental investors."

Macquarie's quantitative equities team also used text-mining techniques in the following research:

- The analysis of changes in the complexity of texts in 10-K reports to predict stock returns. They found that increases in complexity in the management discussion and analysis section of annual reports are associated with future stock underperformance (Macquarie Equities Research 2013a).

- The analysis of 6,000 quarterly conference call transcripts for US companies. They found negligible return drift following an earnings surprise, but changes in tone sentiment were positively related to returns, and the drift lasted up to three months (Macquarie Equities Research 2013b).

- The analysis of press releases for earnings announcements of Russell 3000 Index companies since 2004. They found that combining the soft information embedded in a press release with the release of hard information during the earnings announcement period can be used to enhance the performance of an earnings surprise strategy (Macquarie Equities Research 2014a).

- The analysis of the front page of single-stock fundamental analyst reports prepared by Macquarie. They found that analysts convey significant soft information in their research that is not captured by recommendations, price targets, or fundamental forecasts and that provides insights into fundamental changes (Macquarie Equities Research 2014b).

BlackRock also uses textual analysis to capture alpha. Raffaele Savi and Jeff Shen (2015), co-heads of the firm's Scientific Active Equity Group, write,

> The intense competition in both HFT [high-frequency trading] and long-term investing has led us to increase our research efforts on developing signals that are capable of capturing alpha over an intermediate time frame, measured in days and weeks. ... One such strategy that has proved effective begins with identifying clusters of seemingly unrelated stocks that share common economic return drivers. We then trade within those clusters on a long–short basis when temporary imbalances in investor buy or sell demand cause prices of member stocks to decouple from each other, on the expectation that such dislocations will reverse. To find fundamentally related companies that are not obviously correlated, we employ text-mining algorithms that can interpret vast quantities of written materials, such as company reports, regulatory filings, blogs and social media.

Hafez considers text mining, or natural-language processing (NLP), one of the most disruptive technologies in finance during the past 10–15 years. He observed,

> Ninety percent of all the data in the world has been generated over the last two years, and about 80% of this data comes unstructured—and a large part of this is text based. With the introduction of NLP, suddenly this type of content can be directly incorporated into a (systematic) investment process with little or no human intervention. It all started with news but has expanded into social media, blogs, earnings transcripts, analyst reports, regulatory filings, and such.

An academic attempt to use these technologies to nowcast corporate earnings was made by Kamp, Boley, and Gärtner (2014). They ran data on all S&P 100 Index companies for the 2008–12 period through a fully automated machine-learning method that relies on publicly available data only. Using a simple linear regression based on a novel set of nonnumerical factors that determine market prices, they found that their forecasts could outperform forecasts made by human analysts.

Another example of harnessing computer power to estimate companies' results comes from the Japanese equity research startup Nowcast Inc.[36] Nowcast provides information on consumer prices and retail sales transactions in real time and, using these and other data, provides active managers with automated estimates of the earnings of consumer goods makers. The Tokyo-based firm presently covers 200 Japanese consumer goods companies and has plans to expand that number to about 1,000, including companies in China and the United States. On the macro side, Nowcast couples data from various data sources and advanced analytics to supply real-time inflation numbers and, using nighttime illumination images from satellites as a proxy for real-time economic activity, plans to provide real-time GDP numbers for some of the major world economies in the first half of 2017.

Brar said, "To me, these technologies are of value to fundamental analysts. In the past, analysts used to stand outside stores to measure shopper traffic; now we have more systematic means to do the same."

Expectations and Limitations

Clearly (big) data and advanced analytics have the potential to bring advantages to active managers. The chief investment officer at one quant manager remarked,

---

[36]Nowcast Inc. was formed in 2015 at the University of Tokyo and was subsequently purchased by the Japanese app maker Finatext Ltd.

The traditional active manager with 20–50 stocks will know each one extremely well and will probably have more information than we can hope to have. But we can analyze 5,000 stocks on a consistent basis, whereas a traditional manager using a screen to narrow down his universe will inevitably lose a lot of information.

J.R. Lowry (2016), EMEA head of State Street Global Exchange, writes that he believes that as processes continue to be automated and more information is moved and created online, and as advances in analytic tools allow the accumulation and assessment of the new data, "Some of this data is going to have investable value, and investment managers need to be able to ingest and mine it successfully. However, identifying the right monetisable insights—separating the signal from the noise, so to speak—is a significant challenge."

An example of the challenge comes from what is called the "Hathaway effect." Reportedly, when the American actress Anne Hathaway is in the news, Berkshire Hathaway's stock price receives a boost. In 2015, students at the University of Kansas School of Business ("Finance Students" 2015) were tasked with analyzing whether trading algorithms could be misled by irrelevant information. Focusing on news coverage of the actress and the returns of Berkshire Hathaway's stocks, students found no correlation between news and the price or volatility of the stock, but they did find a positive correlation with trading volumes.

Marcos López de Prado, a senior managing director for Guggenheim Partners and a research fellow at Lawrence Berkeley National Laboratory, cautioned, "Big data, machine learning, and supercomputing require new skills. A blind application of machine learning to large financial datasets will surely result in false discoveries."

Also at the forefront of applying big data and machine learning in investment management, Man AHL's Ledford also cautioned about expectations, saying, "There is no free lunch here: adequate identification of a machine learning model may require extremely large datasets that are, in practice, larger than history allows."

Which raises the question, What are the true capabilities and limits of these technologies? Clearly, analysts can now interact with machines using natural languages and search large databases of texts asking questions formulated in natural languages. Computers equipped with algorithms now seem capable of replacing humans in almost every job, learning from data and discovering relationships better than humans can.

But computers and their algorithms implement step-by-step procedures whereas human mental activities, such as making connections or drawing conclusions, are not done consciously following a step-by-step procedure.

In the twentieth century, mathematicians trying to represent all mathematical reasoning as a step-by-step procedure soon discovered limits to this approach. Some limits are theoretical—for example, limits in machines' ability to perform chains of inference—while other limits are practical. Even if we can state some problems mathematically, they are not necessarily solvable in a finite time by any computer. For example, many optimization problems in finance and economics imply computations that are simply too long to be performed.

Thus, a first limitation to the use of machine learning is simply that not all problems can be easily stated mathematically—and not all problems that can be stated mathematically can be computed.

Learning is a case in point. Machine learning is not what we call "learning" in daily life and in higher mental activities but is essentially a process of minimization of a cost function. Machines learn by minimizing a cost function that has been preprogrammed. They can learn to mimic examples as close as possible (supervised learning) or can learn to find a structure in data (unsupervised learning). In both cases, learning is essentially a process of the minimization of some function. For example, a machine can learn to separate a set of stocks into groups, maximizing the similarity in each group and the dissimilarity between groups, and to recognize price patterns that might be profitable.

A second limitation to the use of machine learning is the fact that some human processes might simply be too complex to be coded into a machine. By forcing all aspects of economic life into a machine-learnable computation, we might actually lose the richness of our thought processes.

Another important point concerns the use of data-mining techniques. What is data mining if not the use of computers to discover patterns in the data? It is an instance of unsupervised learning that creates a mathematical model of data, again (usually) minimizing some function. For example, suppose we want to mine a large dataset of time series—say, 15,000 time series of 100,000 high-frequency price data, plus 100 macroeconomic time series—to discover hidden relationships between these data for investment decision making. Data mining works by assuming a general model of the possible relationships, with possibly a large number of parameters. Such a model—in principle, a universal model—would discover many hidden relationships, including some that are spurious (random). To avoid discovering purely random relationships, the data-mining model is constrained.

This method was popular in the late 1980s with the arrival of the first low-cost supercomputers, and it soon became apparent that the risk of discovering spurious patterns is high. Now, in applying data-mining techniques to much larger datasets, researchers may need to place even stronger constraints on models so that patterns discovered are significant, not spurious, or else take a different approach.

The level of complexity in the financial services sector presents another problem. RavenPack's Hafez observed,

> Today, the various artificial intelligence methodologies are mostly used as part of the data preprocessing stage to produce various analytics or insights from unstructured content rather than in the actual investment process itself. One of the main reasons for this is that finance is a more complex space than most other sectors. It can generally be characterized as involving incomplete information, non-stationarity, and having fuzzy objectives. Today, machine learning can hardly distinguish cats from dogs in a picture if one adds just a bit of "noise." Financial markets are magnitudes more complex.

Macquarie's Brar commented on some of the downsides of using big data and advanced analytics, saying,

> One example: If we only focus on the outputs and don't understand the inputs (i.e., the data), the quality of data and how it is being applied, etc., we will fall into the trap of GIGO [garbage in, garbage out]. Moreover, if we don't build a hypothesis and only interpret the outputs, then again we're at risk. We've always had (big) data, but the key is having an inquisitive mind and knowing what questions to ask.

Another consideration comes from Ledford: "Whilst the machine-learning tools and the inferred knowledge are quantitatively expressed, as for any model, they may just be inputs within a wider qualitative framework."

That framework is the process of fundamental valuation and valuation models. According to Lleo, although we are still at an early stage in understanding how to use these new tools, machine learning will

> dramatically increase the speed at which this [valuation] analysis is performed, broaden the range of information used to forecast cash flows and estimate the cost of capital, increase the breadth and depth of scenarios considered, and upgrade the visualization of the results, thanks to interactive drill-down reports.

Among other effects these tools will have on the valuation and portfolio construction process, Lleo mentioned that machine learning will do the following:

- Bring greater coherence to the valuation of firms within an industry, country, and internationally, with more powerful learning algorithms to limit discrepancies in valuation between firms and countries. This benefit is important because investment has broadened from a domestic, national environment to an international multiasset environment.

- Move from a target price to a target range by broadening the spectrum of scenarios considered in the valuation exercise, thanks to the variety of assumptions one can consider and visualization techniques.

- Connect valuation and portfolio management more closely than in the past. A range of valuations gives a distribution of returns for each asset, complete with a distribution structure that can be used directly in a port-folio optimization model (perhaps toward a greater use of forecasted data as opposed to historical data in portfolio optimization).

But will all investment management firms be able to profit from big data and these tools? Brar commented, "Building such tools and applications requires huge upfront costs—people, data, management commitment—and real benefits would be realized in the future." Already today, one-third (33.6%) of the €56.3 trillion in 2016 global assets managed by the Top 400 asset management firms is managed by just the top 10 firms (Kennedy 2016).

Hafez agreed that the upfront costs are high but suggested alternatives to in-house development:

> It takes a serious investment in infrastructure to build and maintain these systems in-house. The work involved in bringing in raw content and clean-ing it is nontrivial. It requires serious investments in data acquisition, ven-dor management, IT infrastructure, service maintenance, natural-language expertise, and so on. Today, even the most sophisticated quantitative hedge funds and asset managers are outsourcing the work to various data and analytics providers, like Thomson Reuters, Bloomberg, or RavenPack. We already see some firms combining in-house expertise with unstructured-to-structured content from external providers.

Impact of Big Data and AI in Asset Management

How will big data and advanced analytical techniques affect the skills needed by the analyst, investment strategies, and the industry in general?

López de Prado manages $15 billion in internal funds for Guggenheim Partners, where he directs a team of 30 mathematicians and computer sci-entists who apply (exclusively) machine-learning methods. Commenting on their approach, he said,

> We apply a rigorous scientific process to the research, testing, and deploy-ment of investment strategies. Having more people would make us less effective—and might compromise some of our trading secrets. Five years

ago, it would have been unthinkable for such a small group of people, with no background in finance, to manage this amount of money. Machine learning and supercomputing are changing finance. In 10 years' time, finance will have more to do with computer science than economics.

As for the analyst, Lleo remarked, "All of these changes will have an impact on the skill set of financial analysts. The way in which CFA charterholders work in 10–15 years may be very different from the way they work now."

All these changes will also likely reduce the number of analysts (and other personnel) in asset management. In a recent report on the use of data and AI in the financial services industry, Pierron (2017) estimated that these new tools will result in a loss of more than 110,000 jobs in asset and private wealth management between now and 2025. However, analysts also have a marketing function at asset management firms: They help establish the credibility of the firm regarding its claim to be able to generate above-market returns.

Macquarie's Brar commented on the impact of these technologies on investment strategies:

> If these signals help gain competitive advantage—extract alpha or execution—then these innovations will be a disruptive force. The impact will be greater in less-developed markets, but one cannot ignore sophisticated markets like the United States, in which gaining a basis point matters to overall fund performance.

As for the impact of these technologies on the industry as a whole, Brar added,

> Investors who build good platforms and systems will gain a competitive edge, whilst others will have to try to enhance their investment process across other dimensions to maintain their competitive edge. It is too early to say whether the cost/benefit ratio is or will be positive in the future. However, it will be very difficult for an active manager not to be in this space.

RavenPack's Hafez believes that the emergence of alternative data will affect all investment styles, active and passive; all investment strategies, including value and momentum, among others; and all investable universes. He remarked,

> These new technologies can be expected to support both the smart-beta strategies as well as help active investors keep their competitive edge. On the active side, more data creates more opportunities to find new alpha sources, and the future winners in the active (systematic) space will be those who manage to process the most data, most efficiently. The idea of creating

hundreds of thousands, or even millions, of weak learners (or alphas) seems to be part of the winning formula within future quant investing. Of course, there is still the other side of the coin, with a strong hypothesis-driven investment process, combining fundamental domain expertise with the support of alternative data sources—that is to say, using a human overlay on data to alleviate noise.

Hafez added that although alternative data and AI are finding value in US large-capitalization names, the most potential will be found among companies or markets where information is harder to come by or simply not trusted, such as in small-cap stocks or emerging markets. As for geographical take-up, Hafez remarked that while most alternative data available today are for US companies, facilitating the use of AI methodologies on these firms, Europe is catching up, though language differences mean that datasets are more dispersed. He added that interest is high in developing the data and analytical tools for handling information in Chinese and Japanese.

Is all the talk of big data and AI in asset management a return to the technology hype that led to the dot-com bubble? Sorensen cited a recent study by Citi Research (2017) on the business of big data. Referring to the study, Sorensen said,

> It is big in dollars and big in space. Much of it must be stored and processed on the cloud. The list of providers covers considerable breadth—satellite imagery, credit card data, and clicks, to name a few. Rumor has it that the self-identified big-data firms total in the hundreds and reportedly generate an aggregate $50 billion in revenue annually.

Only time will separate hype from reality.

6. Equity Valuation: Does It, Can It Fulfill Its Promise?

Asset managers put time and money into their promise to deliver above-market returns to their clients. They use equity analysts to undertake fundamental analysis and develop valuation models to identify mispricings. Their investment decisions are based on the belief that under- and overpriced assets will revert to some mean or fair value within a given period of time. The expectation is that the manager will then deliver on its promise.

But does the manager deliver? Ever since Burton G. Malkiel, then an economics professor (now emeritus professor) at Princeton University, penned *A Random Walk Down Wall Street* in 1973, the argument has been raging as to whether equity analysts and active management add value.

A frequently used way to address the question is to look at mutual fund returns relative to benchmark funds. However, a caveat is in order. Mutual fund performance available to researchers is limited to returns based on historical price and dividend data. A fund's beta and return volatility are computed from historical returns. Given historical returns, computed return volatility, the estimated beta, and the benchmark, a fund manager's relative performance is determined. The problem is that a fund's return is determined by several activities performed by the fund's management team. Typically, for internal evaluation purposes, a fund does not naively look at only the return and some risk measure to assess the skills of the members of its management team. Rather, some type of performance attribution analysis is used for internal purposes by the financial manager and the trustees.

The most basic equity performance attribution model considers the contribution of three activities: security selection, sector allocation, and market timing (i.e., adjusting beta on the basis of a market view). Assuming that the estimated beta is correct and adjusted for comparing performance against a benchmark, the market-adjusted relative performance would be attributable to either security selection or sector allocation. Thus, equity valuation models may lead to superior selection of stocks within a sector, but an inferior allocation among sectors would result in overall underperformance.

With that caveat in mind, consider the S&P Indices Versus Active (SPIVA) Scorecards, starting with actively managed large-cap funds. As **Table 6.1** illustrates, active large-cap funds in Europe, Japan, and the United States consistently underperform the S&P large-cap indexes in their

Table 6.1. Percentage of Large-Cap Funds That Under- and Outperformed Their Market Benchmark over One-, Three-, and Five-Year Periods Ending 31 December 2016

Market	Benchmark Index	One-Year Performance		Trailing Three-Year Performance		Trailing Five-Year Performance	
		Under	Out	Under	Out	Under	Out
Europe	S&P Europe 350	80%	20%	74%	26%	74%	26%
Japan	S&P TOPIX 150	64%	36%	60%	40%	74%	26%
USA	S&P 500	66%	34%	93%	7%	88%	12%

Source: Constructed by the authors using data obtained from SPIVA (http://us.spindices.com/SPIVA/#/).

respective markets, whether the results are looked at over a one-year, three-year, or five-year period.

Active underperformance relative to S&P indexes is even greater in mid- and small-cap markets, where companies typically benefit from less (sell-side) research than do large-cap firms. **Table 6.2** provides data from the United States as an example.

Although active managers as a group fail to outperform large-, mid-, and small-cap indexes in developed countries, can they do better in emerging-market equities? Some, including Lukas Daadler, chief of investment solutions at the Dutch asset manager Robeco Institutional Asset Management, believe they can. Daadler told *IPE Magazine* journalist Christopher O'Dea (2016) that using market multiples, including price-to-book ratios and P/Es, Robeco estimates that emerging-market stocks are undervalued, perhaps by as much as 25%–30% compared with the MSCI World Index. This gap may provide an opportunity for equity analysts and active managers to add value.

Table 6.2. Percentage of US Active Funds That Under- and Outperformed Their Size-Relevant Market Benchmark over One-, Three-, and Five-Year Periods Ending 31 December 2016

Size Category	Benchmark Index	One-Year Performance		Trailing Three-Year Performance		Trailing Five-Year Performance	
		Under	Out	Under	Out	Under	Out
Midcap	S&P MidCap 400	89%	11%	94%	6%	90%	10%
Small Cap	S&P SmallCap 600	86%	14%	96%	4%	97%	3%

Source: Constructed by the authors using data obtained from SPIVA (http://us.spindices.com/SPIVA/#/).

In fact, emerging-market stocks are unlikely to be uniformly undervalued; what is more likely is that significant differences between stocks exist. This gap offers profit opportunities.

Not everyone agrees. In a recent interview with Daniel Ben-Ami (2016), Malkiel said that even in the case of emerging equity markets—generally viewed as less efficient than developed equity markets—passive managers generally outperform active managers. The only exception he had found, Malkiel said, were local markets in China, where insider trading is said to be common.

Could not only individual analysts but also analysts as a group, from different regions of the world, differ in their ability to forecast stock prices? Comparing analyst performance in both buy and sell recommendations, Harvey, Radnor, Mohammed, and Ferreira (2013) found that Asian analysts—in particular, Japanese analysts—outperform both European and US analysts. Asian analysts made profitable forecasts on both buy and sell recommendations. The authors exclude the efficiency of markets as an explanation but offer no alternative explanation. Might the data, the analytics, be part of the analyst's skill?

Sébastien Lleo, professor of finance at NEOMA Business School (France), remarked that ever since Jensen first looked at mutual fund performance in 1968, financial markets have been grappling with two key questions: (1) What is the value of active management? and (2) Does this value justify its cost? Lleo observed,

> Equity markets in developed economies are open and competitive, and this makes them hard to beat on a risk-adjusted basis over the long term. The results in studies of active management performance are also sensitive to the period under consideration. In addition, the studies generally use the same broad market index to gauge the performance of all the funds, rather than the fund's stated investment benchmark. While the S&P 500 may be the stated benchmark for some active mutual fund managers, others may have different benchmarks, such as the Russell 2000, because they have different strategies and emphasis. And other managers may not have benchmarks at all.

> For example, Warren Buffett famously resisted pressure from shareholders to make the S&P 500 Berkshire Hathaway's benchmark. Although the performance of the S&P 500 now features in Berkshire Hathaway's annual report, Buffett made it clear that it was for information only and that it did not reflect the strategy of the firm. Overall, ignoring the manager's true benchmark will bias the results of the studies.

Still, the dialectic between cost and performance has shaped the investment industry, driving the explosion in the number of hedge funds in the 2000s, the boom in purely passive ETFs [exchange-traded funds], and now the rise in smart-beta ETFs and alternative-beta funds. Each of these successive designs provides a very different set of answers to the two original questions of the value and cost/benefit of active management. Right now, smart beta and alternative beta have anchored the debate in the "low-cost" camp, without giving up on the dream that a strategy (or small set of strategies) can systematically beat the market on a risk-adjusted basis over the long run.

The role of behavioral biases in explaining (under)performance was underlined by Dean Mcintyre, director of performance strategy at FactSet. Mcintyre (2016) identified two widely recognized biases with an impact on performance: the instinct to follow the herd and the tendency to stick to previous price targets.

Another way of understanding how much value analysts and active management add is to look at persistence in performance. Soe and Poirier (2016) write that according to the S&P Persistence Scorecard for the United States,

> one of the key measurements of successful active management lies in the ability of a manager or a strategy to deliver above-average returns consistently over multiple periods. Demonstrating the ability to outperform peers repeatedly is the only proven way to differentiate a manager's luck from skill. According to the S&P Persistence Scorecard, relatively few funds can consistently stay at the top. Out of 631 domestic equity funds that were in the top quartile as of September 2014, only 2.85% managed to stay in the top quartile at the end of September 2016. Furthermore, 2.46% of the large-cap funds, 2.20% of the mid-cap funds, and 3.36% of the small-cap funds remained in the top quartile. For the three-year period that ended in September 2016, persistence figures for funds in the top half were equally unfavorable. Over three consecutive 12-month periods, 18.07% of large-cap funds, 22.95% of mid-cap funds, and 20.88% of small-cap funds maintained a top-half ranking.

> An inverse relationship generally exists between the measurement time horizon and the ability of top-performing funds to maintain their status. It is worth noting that less than 1% of large-cap funds and no mid-cap or small-cap funds managed to remain in the top quartile at the end of the five-year measurement period. This figure paints a negative picture regarding the lack of long-term persistence in mutual fund returns. Similarly, only 4.47% of large-cap funds, 3.68% of mid-cap funds, and 9.27% of small-cap funds maintained top-half performance over five consecutive 12-month periods. Random expectations would suggest a repeat rate of 6.25%.

We can also look at the equilibrium between the cost and the gains of active management by considering *how much information equity analysts add*. At the macro level, one might well ask: Have markets been kept (quasi) efficient, thanks to the combined action of active managers? Up until just 10 years ago, 84% of US mutual fund and ETF assets were actively invested, though the figure had fallen to 66% by the end of 2016.[37] Is evidence available of a change of efficiency during this period?

"No," said Alfred Slager, professor of pension fund management at TIAS School for Business and Society and trustee at the Dutch pension fund for general practitioners SPH:

> The argument is that with less money in active funds, there are fewer transactions, more information asymmetries, and thus more active opportunities. But we observe fewer active managers, more transaction volume, and similarly disappointing active results. So, this argument does not hold. We need to adapt our view of efficiency and financial markets.

> I would suggest the application of the Market Segmentation Theory from the fixed-income realm.[38] Long-term investors are typically buy-and-hold investors who have a different supply-and-demand schedule than the ETF, HFT [high-frequency trading], or insurance company sectors. Depending on the distribution of the security in the different segments, one could hypothesize whether it has become more liquid or not and whether that indicator of efficiency has any meaning.

Concerning how much information equity analysts add—and its value to investors—a recent article in the *Economist* ("Breaking Up Is Hard to Do" 2017) had some unkind words for the sell-side research bundled in banks' services to asset managers:

> At present, banks blast their clients' inboxes with thousands of reports, only a fraction of which are read. The problem is that most research is not very useful—it is hard to come up with original insights about big companies when dozens of other researchers are trying to do the same.

---

[37]Morningstar via the *Wall Street Journal* (18 October 2016).

[38]According to *Investopedia*: "Market segmentation theory is a fundamental theory regarding interest rates and yield curves, expressing the idea that there is no inherent relationship between the levels of short-term and long-term rates. According to market segmentation theory, the prevailing interest rates for short-term, intermediate-term and long-term bonds should be viewed separately, as items in different markets for debt securities. The major conclusion drawn from market segmentation theory and applied to investing is that yield curves are determined by supply and demand forces within each separate market, or category, of debt security maturities, and that the yields for one category of maturities cannot be used to predict the yields for securities within a different maturity market" (www.investopedia.com/terms/m/market-segmentation-theory.asp#ixzz4iTuVfVej).

Citing estimates from Frost Consulting that sell-side equity research budgets have almost halved in the past eight years—going from \$8.2 billion in 2008 to \$4 billion in 2016—and estimates from the research firm Coalition that research jobs are down at banks by around 10% since 2012, the article refers to a "secular decline" in banks' equity research operations. Some of this decline is attributed to new European financial regulations (MiFID [Markets in Financial Instruments Directive] 2) that will force an unbundling of banks' services to asset managers as of January 2018.

Bradford Cornell, professor of financial economics at the California Institute of Technology, challenged the equation of market efficiency with the inability of active managers to outperform passive indexes. In a recent blog post, Cornell (2016) recalled work in the early 1980s by Richard Roll and himself (Cornell and Roll 1981) and by Sanford J. Grossman and Joseph E. Stiglitz (1980) demonstrating that markets can never be fully efficient; efficiency, he remarked, is not the result of some natural phenomenon but the result of research by fundamental investors. He added,

> If those fundamental investors cannot earn a fair rate of return on the resources they put into investment research they will cut back. But as fundamental investors cut back and indexing becomes more common, prices will begin to diverge from fair value making investment research more profitable. As a result, economic theory predicts that the market must be sufficiently inefficient to allow at least sophisticated investors to earn a fair return on their efforts by identifying mispriced securities.

Cornell (2016) cited William Sharpe's argument that equating market efficiency with the inability of active managers as a group to outperform passive indexes is a mistake. Sharpe's proof, Cornell wrote, is as follows:

> Divide investors into two groups: passive investors who hold the market index and active investors who engage in research in an attempt to beat the market. Suppose that in a given year the return on the market index is 10%. By definition passive investors who index the market will also earn 10%. But that means that active investors, as a group must also earn 10%, *before costs*. Given the costs of active investing, active investors as a group must always do worse than passive investors. As Sharpe stresses, this result has nothing to do with market efficiency—it is an arithmetic identity. Even in the most wildly inefficient market, passive investors as a group would still outperform active investors, as a group, taking account of costs and fees. What is true is that if the market is highly efficient, so that few securities are mispriced, there is likely to be little superior or inferior performance *among* the class of active investors. Conversely, if the market is more inefficient, then the more sophisticated investors, who can identify mispriced securities, will benefit at the expense of less informed active investors.

Cornell suggested that for investors who think they have the skill to identify mispriced securities, knowing whether the current movement toward indexing has led to increased market inefficiency would be nice. He explained,

> Ideally, there would be an index of market efficiency that investors could use to judge how likely it would be to find mispriced securities. Unfortunately, there is no such index and there is not likely to be one in the foreseeable future. Asset prices are so volatile and market conditions are so variable that a reasonable index of "inefficiency" cannot be constructed. That is why, 50 years after Eugene Fama introduced the idea of market efficiency, scholars are still arguing about how efficient the market is. There is no evidence that the debate is subsiding. While conceptually it follows that the move toward passive investing will lead to greater inefficiency, whether there has been any material change in market efficiency thus far is unknown.

Some have suggested that if active managers accounted for as little as 10% of the market, efficiency would still be assured. If so, active investors as a group will have performance problems for some time.

Keeping the market price aligned with a firm's intrinsic value is widely considered a key economic role of the fundamental analyst. So, fundamental analysts play an important role in enhancing a firm's access to capital and its ability to invest. Derrien and Kecskés (2013), expanding on previous studies, provided empirical evidence that a decrease in analyst coverage increases information asymmetry. They found that companies that lose an analyst decrease their investment and financing by up to 2% of total assets compared with similar companies that do not lose an analyst. Perhaps not surprisingly, they found that results were stronger for small companies and those with less analyst coverage.

Equity Valuation in a Radically Changed Environment: Does It Retain Its Value?

Graham and Dodd wrote their seminal book *Security Analysis: Principles and Techniques* in 1934. Some 20 years later, roughly 4% of the US population owned stocks. Another 40 years later, that figure had grown fivefold: 20% of the US population owned stocks (including stock mutual funds), thanks largely to the introduction of individual retirement accounts (1974) and the first index funds (1976). The investable universe was still largely domestic and small: 2,670 listed firms in the United States in 1975, according to the World Bank. According to the same database, only 1,398 firms were listed in Japan in 1975, 471 in Germany, and none in either China or India. By 2016, the number of listed firms worldwide had exploded to 43,192, of which only

4,331, or 10%, were in the United States; China (3,052) and India (5,820) together accounted for 20% of all listed firms worldwide. The number of listed firms for Germany in 2016 was 555 and for Japan 3,504.[39]

As discussed in Chapter 5, new technologies are accelerating the analysis and trading of stocks worldwide. Not only has the number of stocks greatly increased because of emerging markets and globalization, but the investable universe has also significantly expanded to include products other than equities. Investors looking for returns have many more options than they did only two or three decades ago. This development raises the question of how returns will be produced in such a changed scenario. Does fundamental analysis retain its central role?

Slager answers "yes and no." He explained,

> Expanding the investment universe increases the need to analyze overall market valuations and the differences and commonalities between them. So, on an aggregate level, fundamental analysis helps. On an individual level, I would not be interested in whether the best security would be picked; "fit-for-purpose" would be fine too. By fit-for-purpose, my idea would be—besides the fact that the company is financially viable—that governance is in order, shareholder rights are protected, and especially ESG [environmental, social, and governance] factors have been taken into consideration. All are crucial for long-term risk management. I sort of suspect that ESG is a form of DNA or fingerprint of the organization and in that sense, might have more predictive value than financials.

Kenneth Little, managing director of the investments group at Brandes Investment Partners, said,

> We believe fundamental analysis can and should retain its central role in investment management, despite the wave of new investment vehicles and strategies over the past few decades. A key function of capital markets is providing for the efficient allocation of capital throughout the economy. We believe fundamental analysis is required to determine which companies deserve (or do not deserve) capital, and their share prices should adjust accordingly.

He added, "While the growth in popularity of index investing (and ETFs that track the indexes) has led to tremendous growth in assets in these vehicles, it has done little to improve the efficient allocation of capital within the respective markets."

---

[39]For more information, see World Bank data on listed companies worldwide (http://data.worldbank.org/indicator/CM.MKT.LDOM.NO?locations=IN-CN-DE-JP-US).

Matteo Bonaventura, a buy-side financial analyst at Banor SIM in Milan, also believes that equity analysis retains its central role. He cited examples from the Italian stock exchange, Borsa Italiana, over the 2007–17 period, during which some underresearched companies realized returns of 500%. But equally important, he noted, is the need for fundamental analysis at several levels, not just the firm level: "A stock market is a mirror of the country, so understanding at least the fundamentals of the country and of the business is crucial."

Bradford Cornell, a professor of financial economics at the California Institute of Technology, believes that "fundamental valuation remains the core of investing. It's central to market pricing and, thereby, capital allocation." Anyone interested in investing, he believes, should master discounted cash flow analysis.

The discussion about the relative importance of asset allocation and active management has changed since the publication of Brinson, Hood, and Beebower's (1986) paper on the determinants of portfolio performance. Their paper was generally taken to have established the dominant role (90%) of asset allocation in explaining equity returns. The role of active management was reasserted 24 years later by Xiong, Ibbotson, Idzorek, and Chen (2010). They pointed out (1) that the 1986 Brinson et al. paper did not study performance but rather variation in performance between one fund and another and (2) that if general market movements (which they found were responsible for about 70% of variation in performance) were excluded, the variation in time-series returns is explained almost equally by asset allocation and active management (16% versus 14%).

The question remains: Is going through the selection process needed to identify an active manager capable of (consistently) outperforming the market worth the time and effort? A recent report from Greenwich Associates (2016) revealed a shift of emphasis on the part of institutional investors from outperformance relative to a benchmark to asset allocation. The report attributed this shift to market volatility and the large-scale devaluation of equity assets during the time period covered by the study.

Andrew Clare, professor of asset management at Cass Business School in London and a pension fund trustee, believes that for many pension fund trustees, searching for the best active managers is not worth the effort. Other decisions, Clare told *IPE Magazine* journalist Carlo Svaluto Moreolo (2016), particularly those relating to asset allocation, are likely to make a far greater difference to overall investment returns: "It's just [that] the amount of difference it [active equity investing] can really make is, for many trustees, not worth the time needed to monitor those things carefully."

Jaap van Dam, principal director of investment strategy at PGGM Investments, the €200 billion Dutch pension fund for health and social workers, voiced a similar opinion. He said, "If you look at aggregated results of pension funds globally, there is a small contribution from active management to the total return, and only if it is well controlled for cost." PGGM is reviewing its bottom-up investment decision-making processes. "We now want more discussion on understanding where and how value is created and transformed into profits," Van Dam said. "We believe in creating value by looking at the fundamentals of value creation over the long term."

A New Role for Fundamental Analysis in Asset Management?

Can equity analysts and active managers find a new role for themselves?

Given past performance records, Axel Pierron, co-founder and co-managing director of the financial consultancy firm Opima, was somewhat pessimistic about active management's ability to compete on alpha generation. He said,

> If you look at passive investment vehicles that are gaining market share, such as ETFs, BlackRock has 50% of the market in Europe. Branding is becoming very important. If you don't have brand recognition, you might try to focus on alpha, but it is not so easy. Regulation in Europe that imposes benchmarking will have an impact. Without strong performance, an asset manager will need a strong brand or to be part of a large retail bank. Independent asset managers will find it harder to acquire and keep assets.

Looking over the past two decades—which saw the emergence of, first, hedge funds and, more recently, smart-beta ETFs—in answering the questions of whether active management adds value and whether it is worth the cost, Lleo remarked,

> The rise of robo-advisors may change this emphasis again by transforming active management into a dynamic, client-focused process, in which the ultimate objective in constituting a portfolio is not to beat the market but to deliver results consistent with the goals and psychology of the investor.

Beyond psychology, Marc Reinganum, a former senior managing director at State Street Global Advisors, suggests,

Outcome-centric investing is on the ascent. Outcomes are future consumption or spending streams and should be treated as future liabilities. The goal of an outcome-oriented strategy should be to match or exceed changes in the present values of the liabilities with minimum return deviations between the liabilities and the assets that are funding the liabilities.

Pascal Blanqué, chief investment officer and head of institutional business at the French asset management group Amundi, suggested that the time has come for active managers to shift the accent from stock picking to asset allocation. Blanqué (2016) writes:

> The role of active managers is increasingly challenged, as far as stock picking is concerned; nevertheless, it maintains a highly important role in asset allocation. Even sophisticated investors with a strong asset allocation expertise show increasing interest in innovative asset allocation methods and processes, with a preference for absolute-return over more traditional benchmark approaches. As a result, we are convinced that the distinction between active and passive management is becoming less clear-cut.
>
> The role of active management has not disappeared; its focus has just shifted over time. The choice of factors and weighting schemes and the search for value through asset allocation are all active decisions that investors must now focus on. For asset managers, the challenge is therefore to provide a combination of a wide range of passive vehicles and of selected active expertise with proven alpha, with a strong capacity to accompany clients in their asset allocation decisions and in the efficient execution of the latter.

In a similar vein, Slager had several suggestions as to how active managers might increase their value to (institutional) investors:[40]

> From a pension fund perspective, I see that in Europe, classic active strategies are being eschewed, and passive is on the rise. At the same time, in discussions with trustees, the picture emerges that active strategies have an added value, just not in the somewhat antiquated "let's beat the benchmark" form. Some ideas that have emerged from recent discussions include using active managers to work on developing a new set of metrics. What sort of strategy would best aid the pension funds' goals? Which risk factors would one add, compared to the total portfolio?
>
> In other words, linking to the integral objectives, not sticking to isolated carve-outs in the investment portfolio, should shape future investment strategies. Other ideas include replacing the classical, highly bureaucratic "Request for Proposal" with the opportunity for active managers to present

---

[40]See also Koedijk and Slager (2011).

truly relevant business cases for their active management strategies. Active managers could innovate on testing strategy introduction: How could we emulate prototyping, testing, and the introduction of a new strategy in such a way that it filters out the mediocre strategies from the start? Moving from the classical database backtesting to live simulation raises the hurdle but increases the chances of *designing durable investment strategies*, and of a long-term partnership. Trustees would no longer be drawn into overly technical asset pricing discussions but could focus on what matters—will active management work?

References

Aggarwal, Rajesh, Sanjai Bhagat, and Srinivasan Rangan. 2009. "The Impact of Fundamentals on IPO Valuation." *Financial Management*, vol. 38, no. 2 (Summer): 253–284.

Allan, Gareth, and Komaki Ito. 2016. "Fintech Venture Targets Hedge Funds with Big-Data Research." Bloomberg (12 September; updated 13 September): www.bloomberg.com/news/articles/2016-09-13/fintech-startup-dives-into-big-data-for-japanese-stock-research.

Almeida, Robert M., Jr. 2016. "Decision Drivers: Stock Prices versus GDP." MFS White Paper Series (October): www.mfs.com/content/dam/mfs-enterprise/pdfs/thought-leadership/us/mfse_gdp_wp.pdf.

Ang, Andrew, and Geert Bekaert. 2007. "Stock Return Predictability: Is It There?" *Review of Financial Studies*, vol. 20, no. 3 (May): 651–707.

Appelbaum, Eileen, and Rosemary Batt. 2016 (updated March 2017). "Are Lower Private Equity Returns the New Normal?" Center for Economic and Policy Research (June): http://cepr.net/publications/reports/are-lower-private-equity-returns-the-new-normal.

Bajo, Emanuel, Thomas J. Chemmanur, Karen Simonyan, and Hassan Tehranian. 2016. "Underwriter Networks, Investor Attention, and Initial Public Offerings." *Journal of Financial Economics*, vol. 122, no. 2 (November): 376–408.

Barra/MSCI. 2010. "Is There a Link between GDP Growth and Equity Returns?" (May): www.msci.com/documents/10199/a134c5d5-dca0-420d-875d-06adb948f578.

Beck, Ulrich. 1992. *Risk Society: Toward a New Modernity*, English ed. London: SAGE Publications.

Ben-Ami, Daniel. 2016. "Active Management: The Active-Passive Debate." *IPE Magazine* (January): www.ipe.com/reports/active-managemet/special-report-active-management-the-active-passive-debate/10011319.article.

Bindseil, Ulrich, and Philipp J. König. 2013. "Basil J. Moore's *Horizontalists and Verticalists*: An Appraisal 25 Years Later." *Review of Keynesian Economics*, vol. 1, no. 4 (Winter): 383–390.

Birstingl, Andrew. 2016. "Initial Public Offerings: Q4 2016 Highlights." *FactSet IPO Quarterly* (December): https://insight.factset.com/hubfs/Insight/Migration/IPO%20Quarterly/IPO%20Quarterly%20Q4%202016_12.29.pdf.

BlackRock. 2016. "Global Investment Outlook: Q2 2016." BlackRock Investment Institute (www.blackrock.com/corporate/en-ca/literature/white-paper/bii-global-investment-outlook-q2-2016-us.pdf).

Blanqué, Pascal. 2016. "Asset Allocation Is an Active Process." *IPE Magazine* (January): www.ipe.com/reports/special-reports/active-management/pension-funds-what-role-for-active-management/10011322.article.

Bonaventura, Matteo, and Giancarlo Giudici. 2016. "IPO Valuation and Profitability Expectations: Evidence from the Italian Exchange." *Eurasian Business Review*, vol. 7, no. 2: 247–266.

"Breaking Up Is Hard to Do: Banks' Equity-Research Operations Are in Decline." 2017. *Economist* (30 March): www.economist.com/news/finance-and-economics/21719829-unable-give-their-research-away-they-will-struggle-find-buyers-it-banks.

Brettell, Karen, David Gaffen, and David Rohde. 2015a. "As Stock Buybacks Reach Historic Levels, Signs That Corporate America Is Undermining Itself." Part I of "The Cannibalized Company: A Reuters Special Report." Reuters (16 November): https://www.reuters.com/investigates/special-report/usa-buybacks-cannibalized/.

———. 2015b. "Stock Buybacks Enrich the Bosses Even When Business Sags." Part II of "The Cannibalized Company: A Reuters Special Report." Reuters (10 December): https://www.reuters.com/investigates/special-report/usa-buybacks-pay/.

Brinson, Gary P., L. Randolph Hood, and Gilbert L. Beebower. 1986. "Determinants of Portfolio Performance." *Financial Analysts Journal*, vol. 42, no. 4 (July/August): 39–44.

Burke, John. 2016. "4 Reasons for the IPO Market Slowdown in 2016." *Investopedia* (14 June): www.investopedia.com/articles/markets/061416/4-reasons-ipo-market-slowdown-2016-ipo.asp#ixzz4O5vkFSle.

Burns, Dan. 2017. "Ghosts of Past Tech IPOs Could Haunt Snap's Performance." Thomson Reuters (24 February).

Butters, John. 2017. "Highest Forward 12-Month P/E Ratio for S&P since 2004." *FactSet Insight* (17 February): https://insight.factset.com/earningsinsight_02.17.17.

Campbell, J.Y., and R.J. Shiller. 1988. "Stock Prices, Earnings and Expected Dividends." *Journal of Finance*, vol. 43, no. 3 (July): 661–676.

Carey, David, and Devin Banerjee. 2016. "Private Equity's Golden Age Wasn't So Golden after All." Bloomberg (21 January).

Chee, Seungmin, Richard G. Sloan, and Aydin Uysal. 2013. "A Framework for Value Investing." *Australian Journal of Management*, vol. 38, no. 3 (December): 599–633.

Chemmanur, Thomas, and An Yan. 2011. "Advertising, Investor Recognition, and Stock Returns." Working paper (April): http://econ.shufe.edu.cn/upload/htmleditor/Image/74319_1105160822451.pdf.

———. 2017. "Product Market Advertising, Heterogeneous Beliefs, and the Long-Run Performance of Initial Public Offerings." *Journal of Corporate Finance*, vol. 46 (October): 1–24 (www.sciencedirect.com/science/article/pii/S0929119917303899).

Citi Research. 2017. "Searching for Alpha: Big Data: Navigating New Alternative Datasets" (10 March).

Cochrane, John H. 2001 (rev. ed., 2005). *Asset Pricing*. Princeton, NJ: Princeton University Press.

Cornell, Bradford. 2010. "Economic Growth and Equity Investing." *Financial Analysts Journal*, vol. 66, no. 1 (January/February): 54–64.

———. 2014. "Dividend–Price Ratios and Stock Returns: International Evidence." *Journal of Portfolio Management*, vol. 40, no. 2 (Winter): 122–127.

———. 2016. "Market Efficiency and the Impact of Passive Investing." *Brad Cornell's Economics Blog* (7 November): http://wbcornell.blogspot.com/2016/11/market-efficiency-and-impact-of-passive.html.

Cornell, Bradford, and Aswath Damodaran. 2014. "Tesla: Anatomy of a Run-Up." *Journal of Portfolio Management*, vol. 41, no. 1 (Fall): 139–151.

Cornell, Bradford, and Rajiv Gokhale. 2016. "An 'Enhanced Multiple' Corporation Valuation Model: Theory and Empirical Tests." *Business Valuation Review*, vol. 35, no. 2 (Summer): 52–61.

Cornell, Bradford, and Richard Roll. 1981. "Strategies for Pairwise Competitions in Markets and Organizations." *Bell Journal of Economics*, vol. 12, no. 1 (Spring): 201–213.

Costa, Sofia Horta E. 2016. "Market Jolts Make European Buybacks Newest Investor Favorite." Bloomberg (4 February; updated 5 February): www.bloomberg.com/news/articles/2016-02-05/once-pro-dividend-european-shareholders-slowly-warm-to-buybacks.

Credit Suisse. 2017. "It's Always Darkest before Dawn; Key Secular Headwinds Will Start to Improve in 2018–19." Connections Series, Credit Suisse Global Asset Managers (4 May): www.bluetractorgroup.com/uploads/5/7/6/1/57612741/credit_suisse_equity_research_may_2017_mention_of_blue_tractor.pdf.

Damodaran, Aswath. 2005. "The Promise and Peril of Real Options." Working paper, New York University Stern School of Business (July): www.researchgate.net/publication/228142262_The_Promise_and_Peril_of_Real_Options.

————. 2016. "Mean Reversion: Gravitational Super Force or Dangerous Delusion?" *Seeking Alpha* (1 September): https://seekingalpha.com/article/4003590-mean-reversion-gravitational-super-force-dangerous-delusion.

Degeorge, François, François Derrien, and Kent. L. Womack. 2007. "Analyst Hype in IPOs: Explaining the Popularity of Bookbuilding." *Review of Financial Studies*, vol. 20, no. 4 (July): 1021–1058.

DeLong, J. Bradford. 1996. "Is the Stock Market Too High?" *Slate* (22 December): www.slate.com/articles/news_and_politics/the_gist/1996/12/is_the_stock_market_too_high.html.

DeLong, J. Bradford, Andrei Shleifer, Lawrence H. Summers, and Robert J. Waldmann. 1990. "Noise Trader Risk in Financial Markets." *Journal of Political Economy*, vol. 98, no. 4 (August): 703–738.

DeMiguel, Victor, Lorenzo Garlappi, and Raman Uppal. 2009. "Optimal versus Naive Diversification: How Inefficient Is the $1/N$ Portfolio Strategy?" *Review of Financial Studies*, vol. 22, no. 5 (May): 1915–1953.

Derrien, François, and Ambrus Kecskés. 2013. "The Real Effects of Financial Shocks: Evidence from Exogenous Changes in Analyst Coverage." *Journal of Finance*, vol. 68, no. 4 (August): 1407–1440.

Dimson, Elroy, Paul Marsh, and Mike Staunton. 2014. "The Growth Puzzle." In *Credit Suisse Global Investment Returns Yearbook 2014* (February): 17–29 (http://doc.xueqiu.com/14cdbae48e74653fe7546fe0.pdf).

Doidge, Craig, G. Andrew Karolyi, and René M. Stulz. 2015. "The U.S. Listing Gap." NBER Working Paper 21181 (May): www.nber.org/papers/w21181.

Downie, Ryan. 2016. "Is the Private Equity Bubble Still Expanding?" *Investopedia* (15 June): www.investopedia.com/articles/markets/061516/private-equity-bubble-still-expanding-gs.asp#ixzz4O5wFX3QU.

Ernst & Young. 2015. "Positioning to Win: 2015 Global Private Equity Survey" (www.ey.com/gl/en/industries/financial-services/fso-insights-global-private-equity-survey-2015).

———. 2016. "Disruption Causes Seismic Shift for Private Equity: 2016 Global Private Equity Fund and Investor Survey" (www.ey.com/gl/en/industries/private-equity/ey-2016-global-private-equity-fund-and-investor-survey).

Fabozzi, Frank J., K.C. Chen, K.C. Ma, and Jessica West. 2015. "In Search of Cash-Flow Pricing." *Journal of Financial Research*, vol. 38, no. 4 (Winter): 511–527.

Fama, Eugene F. 1970. "Efficient Capital Markets: A Review of Theory and Empirical Work." *Journal of Finance*, vol. 25, no. 2 (May): 383–417.

———. 1976. "Reply." *Journal of Finance*, vol. 31, no. 1 (March): 143–145.

Feldstein, Martin. 2016. "What Could Go Wrong in America?" *Project Syndicate* (26 October): www.project-syndicate.org/commentary/asset-price-risk-in-america-by-martin-feldstein-2016-10.

Fernandez, Pablo. 2002 (rev. 2007). "Company Valuation Methods: The Most Common Errors in Valuation." Working Paper 449, IESE Business School, University of Navarra.

Fernandez, Pablo. 2015. "119 Common Errors in Company Valuations." Working Paper 714, IESE Business School, University of Navarra.

"Fewer Japanese Companies Planning Stock Buybacks: Declining Trend Could Affect Supply–Demand Balance." 2017. *Nikkei Asian Review* (9 February): http://asia.nikkei.com/Markets/Tokyo-Market/Fewer-Japanese-companies-planning-stock-buybacks.

"Finance Students Investigate the 'Hathaway Effect.'" 2015. *KU* (blog), University of Kansas School of Business (25 February): https://blog.business. ku.edu/category/anne-hathaway/.

Foulke, David. 2016. "Value Investing Got Crushed During the Internet Bubble—Here's Why." *Alpha Architect* (blog; 10 October): https://alphaarchitect. com/2016/10/10/value-investing-got-crushed-during-the-internet-bubble-heres-why/.

Gao, Xiaohui, Jay R. Ritter, and Zhongyan Zhu. 2013. "Where Have All the IPOs Gone?" *Journal of Financial and Quantitative Analysis*, vol. 48, no. 6 (December): 1663–1692.

GF Data Resources. 2017. "Have Mid-Market Values Peaked?" (21 February): https://www.gfdata.com/news/articles/have-mid-market-values-peaked/.

Goedhart, Marc, Timothy Koller, and David Wessels. 2005. "The Right Role for Multiples in Valuation." *McKinsey on Finance: Perspectives on Corporate Finance and Strategy*, no. 15 (Spring): 7–11 (www.mckinsey. com/business-functions/strategy-and-corporate-finance/our-insights/ the-right-role-for-multiples-in-valuation).

Gompers, Paul, Steven N. Kaplan, and Vladimir Mukharlyamov. 2015. "What Do Private Equity Firms Say They Do?" NBER Working Paper 21133 (April): http://www.nber.org/papers/w21133.

Gompers, Paul, and Josh Lerner. 2000. "Money Chasing Deals? The Impact of Fund Inflows on Private Equity Valuations." *Journal of Financial Economics*, vol. 55, no. 1 (January): 281–325.

Graham, Benjamin. 1949 (4th ed., 1973). *The Intelligent Investor.* New York: Harper & Row.

Graham, Benjamin, and David Dodd. 1934 (1st ed.; 6th ed., 2008). *Security Analysis: Principles and Techniques.* New York: McGraw-Hill.

Grantham, Jeremy. 2017. "This Time Seems Very, Very Different." Part 2 of "Not with a Bang but a Whimper—A Thought Experiment." *GMO Quarterly Letter* (https://seekingalpha.com/article/4068324-time-seems-different-part-2-bang-whimper-thought-experiment).

Gray, Wesley R., and Jack Vogel. 2012. "Analyzing Valuation Measures: A Performance Horse Race over the Past 40 Years." *Journal of Portfolio Management*, vol. 39, no. 1 (Fall): 112–121.

Greenwich Associates. 2016. "Is There a Future for Active Management? How Active Managers Will Thrive in a Maturing Industry" (December).

Greiner, Steven P. 2011. *Ben Graham Was a Quant: Raising the IQ of the Intelligent Investor*. Hoboken, NJ: Wiley.

Grossman, Sanford J., and Joseph E. Stiglitz. 1980. "On the Impossibility of Informationally Efficient Markets." *American Economic Review*, vol. 70, no. 3 (June): 393–408.

Harvey, Campbell R., Sam Radnor, Khalil Mohammed, and William Ferreira. 2013. "Where Are the World's Best Analysts?" Working paper (25 November).

Hillert, Alexander, Heiko Jacobs, and Sebastian Müller. 2014. "Media Makes Momentum." *Review of Financial Studies*, vol. 27, no. 12 (December): 3467–3501.

Ibbotson, Roger G., and Peng Chen. 2003. "Long-Run Stock Returns: Participating in the Real Economy." *Financial Analysts Journal*, vol. 59, no.1 (January/February): 88–98.

Ibbotson, Roger G., Jody L. Sindelar, and Jay R. Ritter. 1994. "The Market's Problems with the Pricing of Initial Public Offerings." *Journal of Applied Corporate Finance*, vol. 7, no. 1 (Spring): 66–74.

Ilmanen, Antti. 2016. "A Historical Perspective on Time-Varying Expected Returns." Chapter 2 in *Financial Market History: Reflections on the Past for Investors Today*, edited by David Chambers and Elroy Dimson. Charlottesville, VA: CFA Institute Research Foundation (www.cfapubs.org/toc/rf/2016/2016/3).

Jacobius, Arleen. 2016. "Private Equity Valuations a Concern for Endowments, Foundations but Are Not Affecting Allocations." *Pensions & Investments* (24 October): www.pionline.com/article/20161024/ONLINE/161029952/.

Jakab, Spencer. 2016. "The Hidden Weaknesses of Index Funds." *Wall Street Journal* (18 October): www.wsj.com/articles/the-hidden-weaknesses-of-index-funds-1476799335.

Jarrow, Robert. 2016. "Asset Price Bubbles and the Land of Oz." *Journal of Portfolio Management*, vol. 42, no. 2 (Winter): 37–42.

Jenkinson, Tim, Miguel Sousa, and Rüdiger Stucke. 2013. "How Fair Are the Valuations of Private Equity Funds?" Working paper (February).

Jensen, Michael C. 1968. "The Performance of Mutual Funds in the Period 1945–1964." *Journal of Finance*, vol. 23, no. 2 (May): 389–416.

Jensen, Niels C. 2015. "The 'Perfect Storm.'" *Absolute Return Letter*, Absolute Return Partners (April): www.arpinvestments.com/arl/the-perfect-storm.

Kamp, Michael, Mario Boley, and Thomas Gärtner. 2014. "Beating Human Analysts in Nowcasting Corporate Earnings by Using Publicly Available Stock Prices and Correlation Features." *Proceedings of the 2014 International Conference on Data Mining* (28 April): 641–649 (http://epubs.siam.org/doi/abs/10.1137/1.9781611973440.74).

Kennedy, Liam. 2016. "Top 400 Asset Managers 2016: Global Assets Now €56.3trn." *IPE Magazine* (June): www.ipe.com/reports/special-reports/top-400-asset-managers/top-400-asset-managers-2016-global-assets-now-563trn/10013542.fullarticle (for the full list, see www.ipe.com/Uploads/d/t/n/Top-400-list-2016.pdf).

Kim, Moonchul, and Jay R. Ritter. 1999. "Valuing IPOs." *Journal of Financial Economics*, vol. 53, no. 3 (September): 409–437.

Kitanaka, Anna, and Toshiro Hasegawa. 2016. "BlackRock Sides with Japan's Central Bank over ETF Buying." Bloomberg (14 September; updated 15 September): www.bloomberg.com/news/articles/2016-09-14/blackrock-sides-with-boj-in-debate-over-tokyo-whale-s-etf-buying.

Koedijk, Kees, and Alfred Slager. 2011. *Investment Beliefs: A Positive Approach to Institutional Investing*. Basingstoke, UK: Palgrave Macmillan.

Kumar, Alok. 2009. "Hard-to-Value Stocks, Behavioral Biases, and Informed Trading." *Journal of Financial and Quantitative Analysis*, vol. 44, no. 6 (December): 1375–1401.

Laubach, Thomas, and John C. Williams. 2015. "Measuring the Natural Rate of Interest Redux." Federal Reserve Bank of San Francisco Working Paper 2015-16 (October): www.frbsf.org/economic-research/publications/working-papers/wp2015-16.pdf.

Ledford, Anthony. n.d. "AHL Explains Machine Learning." Chapter 3 in the AHL Explains series *Maths: The Power to Do Incredible Things*. Oxford, UK: Man AHL (www.ahl.com/insights/machine-learning.INGS).

Lee, Charles M.C. 2003. "Choosing the Right Valuation Approach." *AIMR Conference Proceedings*, vol. 2003, no. 2 (April): 4–14 (http://www.cfapubs.org/doi/abs/10.2469/cp.v2003.n2.3271).

LeRoy, Stephen F. 1976. "Efficient Capital Markets: Comment." *Journal of Finance*, vol. 31, no. 1 (March): 139–141.

Lewis, Leo. 2016. "Corporate Japan Acquires a Buyback Habit." *Financial Times* (21 December): www.ft.com/content/23076ada-c768-11e6-9043-7e34c07b46ef?mhq5j=e6.

L'Her, Jean-François, Rossitsa Stoyanova, Kathryn Shaw, William Scott, and Charissa Lai. 2016. "A Bottom-Up Approach to the Risk-Adjusted Performance of the Buyout Fund Market." *Financial Analysts Journal*, vol. 72, no. 4 (July/August): 36–48.

Liu, Jing, Doron Nissim, and Jacob Thomas. 2002. "Equity Valuation Using Multiples." *Journal of Accounting Research*, vol. 40, no. 1 (March): 135–172 (www0.gsb.columbia.edu/mygsb/faculty/research/pubfiles/318/Equity_Valuation_Using_Multiples.pdf).

———. 2007. "Is Cash Flow King in Valuations?" *Financial Analysts Journal*, vol. 63, no. 2 (March/April): 56–68.

Loomis, Carol. 2001. "Warren Buffett on the Stock Market." *Fortune* (10 December): http://archive.fortune.com/magazines/fortune/fortune_archive/2001/12/10/314691/index.htm.

Lowe, Janet. 2010. *The Triumph of Value Investing: Smart Money Tactics for the Postrecession Era*. New York: Penguin.

Lowry, J.R. 2016. "Top 400: Disruptive Technology—The Four 'Ds' of Disruption." *IPE Magazine* (June): www.ipe.com/reports/special-reports/top-400-asset-managers/top-400-disruptive-technology-the-four-ds-of-disruption/10013553.fullarticle.

Lubik, Thomas A., and Christian Matthes. 2015. "Calculating the Natural Rate of Interest: A Comparison of Two Alternative Approaches." Federal Reserve Bank of Richmond *Economic Brief* (October): https://www.richmondfed.org/-/media/richmondfedorg/publications/research/economic_brief/2015/pdf/eb_15-10.pdf.

Macquarie Equities Research. 2013a. "Camouflaged in Complexity: Using Textual Analysis to Extract Signals from 10-K Reports." *Quantamentals* (6 February).

———. 2013b. "The Price Is Right." *Quantamentals* (29 October): https://www.ravenpack.com/research/quantamentals-the-price-is-right/.

———. 2014a. "A Surprising Tone." *Quantamentals* (10 July).

———. 2014b. "How Are You Really Feeling?" *Quantamentals* (12 November).

———. 2015. "I Just Called to Say I'm Bullish." *Quantamentals* (20 April).

Malkiel, Burton G. 1973 (10th ed., 2012). *A Random Walk Down Wall Street: The Time-Tested Strategy for Successful Investing.* New York: Norton.

Man Group. 2014. "Is Momentum Behavioural?" AHL/MSS Academic Advisory Board group discussion (March): www.man.com/is-momentum-behavioural.

Marenzi, Octavio. 2017. "Alternative Data—The New Frontier in Asset Management." *Opimas* (31 March): www.opimas.com/research/217/detail/.

Mariathasan, Joseph. 2016. "Non-Traditional Investment: Quant versus Traditional." *IPE Magazine* (January): www.ipe.com/reports/special-reports/active-management/non-traditional-investment-quant-versus-traditional/10011326.article.

Mcintyre, Dean. 2016. "Management Performance: Good Behavior or Good Luck?" *FactSet Insight* (22 November): https://insight.factset.com/manager-performance-good-behavior-or-good-luck.

McKinsey Private Equity and Principal Investors Practice. 2017. "McKinsey Global Private Markets Review: A Routinely Exceptional Year." McKinsey & Company (February): www.mckinsey.com/~/media/McKinsey/Industries/Private%20Equity%20and%20Principal%20Investors/Our%20Insights/A%20routinely%20exceptional%20year%20for%20private%20equity/McKinsey-Global-Private-Markets-Review-February-2017.ashx.

McLeay, Michael, Amar Radia, and Ryland Thomas. 2014a. "Money in the Modern Economy: An Introduction." *Quarterly Bulletin*, Monetary Analysis Directorate of the Bank of England (Q1 2014): www.bankofengland.co.uk/publications/Documents/quarterlybulletin/2014/qb14q101.pdf.

———. 2014b. "Money Creation in the Modern Economy." *Quarterly Bulletin*, Monetary Analysis Directorate of the Bank of England (Q1 2014): www.bankofengland.co.uk/publications/Documents/quarterlybulletin/2014/qb14q102.pdf.

Merton, Robert C. 1974. "On the Pricing of Corporate Debt: The Risk Structure of Interest Rates." *Journal of Finance*, vol. 29, no. 2 (May): 449–470.

Miller, Edward M. 1977. "Risk, Uncertainty, and Divergence of Opinion." *Journal of Finance*, vol. 32, no. 4 (September): 1151–1168.

Montier, James, and Philip Pilkington. 2016. "The Stock Market as Monetary Policy Junkie: Quantifying the Fed's Impact on the S&P 500." GMO white paper (March).

Moore, Basil. 1988. *Horizontalists and Verticalists: The Macroeconomics of Credit Money*. Cambridge, UK: Cambridge University Press.

Moore, Charlotte. 2016. "Time to Become More Active?" *IPE Magazine* (January): www.ipe.com/reports/special-reports/active-management/time-to-become-more-active/10011325.article.

Moreolo, Carlo Svaluto. 2016. "Pension Funds: What Role for Active Management?" *IPE Magazine* (January): www.ipe.com/reports/special-reports/active-management/pension-funds-what-role-for-active-management/10011322.article.

Morningstar Manager Research. 2017. "Morningstar Direct Asset Flows Commentary: United States." Morningstar (11 January): https://corporate.morningstar.com/US/documents/AssetFlows/AssetFlowsJan2017.pdf.

Nath, Trevir. 2016. "Public vs. Private Tech Valuations: What's Driving the Divide?" *Investopedia* (5 February): www.investopedia.com/articles/investing/020516/public-vs-private-tech-valuations-whats-driving-divide.asp#ixzz4O5wesPJO.

Nesbitt, Stephen L. 2016. "An Examination of State Pension Performance: 2006 to 2015" (6 September): www.cliffwater.com/Cliffwater%20Research%20-%20An%20Examination%20of%20State%20Pension%20Performance%202006-2015.pdf.

Nolen Foushee, Susan, Tim Koller, and Anand Mehta. 2012. "Why Bad Multiples Happen to Good Companies." *McKinsey Quarterly* (May): www.mckinsey.it/idee/why-bad-multiples-happen-to-good-companies.

O'Dea, Christopher. 2016. "Valuations: Emerging from the Wings." *IPE Magazine* (October): www.ipe.com/investment/investing-in-global-equities/valuations-emerging-from-the-wings/10015442.article.

O'Neill, Jim, Anna Stupnytska, and James Wrisdale. 2011. "Linking GDP Growth and Equity Returns." *Monthly Insights*, Goldman Sachs Asset Management (May): http://s3.amazonaws.com/zanran_storage/www2.goldmansachs.com/ContentPages/2509459477.pdf.

Paleari, Stefano, Andrea Signori, and Silvio Vismara. 2014. "How Do Underwriters Select Peers When Valuing IPOs?" *Financial Management*, vol. 43, no. 4 (Winter): 731–755.

Penman, Stephen. 2016. "Valuation: The State of the Art." *Schmalenbach Business Review*, vol. 17, no. 1 (April): 3–23.

Pierron, Axel. 2017. "Artificial Intelligence in Capital Markets: The Next Operational Revolution." *Opimas* (1 March): www.opimas.com/research/210/detail/.

Pilkington, Philip. 2014. "Endogenous Money and the Natural Rate of Interest: The Reemergence of Liquidity Preference and Animal Spirits in the Post-Keynesian Theory of Capital Markets." Working Paper 817, Levy Economics Institute of Bard College (September): www.levyinstitute.org/pubs/wp_817.pdf.

Pinto, Jerald E., Thomas R. Robinson, and John D. Stowe. 2015. "Equity Valuation: A Survey of Professional Practice." Working paper, CFA Institute (September): https://papers.ssrn.com/sol3/papers.cfm?abstract_id=2657717.

"Private Equity Valuations: Best Practices and Pitfalls." 2015. Grant Thornton survey (www.grantthornton.com/~/media/content-page-files/private-equity/pdfs/2015/150331-PE-Valuations-whitepaper-150408-FINALB.ashx).

Purnanandam, Amiyatosh K., and Bhaskaran Swaminathan. 2004. "Are IPOs Really Underpriced?" *Review of Financial Studies*, vol. 17, no. 3 (July): 811–848.

"Q&A: Valuations for the Private Equity Industry." 2014. *Financier Worldwide Magazine*, Special Report: Private Equity (September): www.financierworldwide.com/qa-valuations-for-the-private-equity-industry/#.WNJBQPk1_IU.

Rhodes-Kropf, M., David T. Robinson, and S. Viswanathan. 2005. "Valuation Waves and Merger Activity: The Empirical Evidence." *Journal of Financial Economics*, vol. 77, no. 3 (September): 561–603.

Rich, Bryan. 2016. "What Warren Buffett Thinks about Stock Valuations." *Forbes* (26 May): www.forbes.com/sites/bryanrich/2016/05/26/what-warren-buffett-thinks-about-stock-valuations/#6623dcdf1f4b.

Ritter, Jay R. 2005. "Economic Growth and Equity Returns." *Pacific-Basin Finance Journal*, vol. 13, no. 5 (November): 489–503 (https://site.warrington.ufl.edu/ritter/files/2015/04/Economic-growth-and-equity-returns-2005.pdf).

Robeco Institutional Asset Management. 2016. "5-Year Expected Returns, 2018–2022" (www.robeco.com/en/themes/expected-returns/index.html).

Roosenboom, Peter. 2012. "Valuing and Pricing IPOs." *Journal of Banking & Finance*, vol. 36, no. 6 (June): 1653–1664.

Savi, Raffaele, Bill MacCartney, Bradley J. Betts, and Jeff Shen. 2015. "Finding Big Alpha in Big Data: The Evolution of Active Investing." BlackRock white paper (September): www.blackrock.com/institutions/en-axj/literature/market-commentary/finding-big-apha-in-big-data-axj.pdf.

Savi, Raffaele, and Jeff Shen. 2015. "Constant Change, Consistent Alpha: The Innovation Challenge for Active Investors." BlackRock white paper (October): www.blackrock.com/institutions/en-us/literature/whitepaper/blk-constant-change-consistent-alpha.pdf.

Sheridan, Ben, Brent Beardsley, Martin Ouimet, and Elias Baltassis. 2016. "How Asset Managers Can Succeed with Advanced Analytics." Boston Consulting Group (25 July): www.bcgperspectives.com/content/articles/financial-institutions-technology-digital-asset-managers-can-succeed-advanced-analytics/.

Shleifer, Andrei, and Robert W. Vishny. 1997. "The Limits of Arbitrage." *Journal of Finance*, vol. 52, no. 1 (March): 35–55.

Siblis Research. n.d. "Global Market Cap to GNI/GDP Ratios for 28 Countries" (http://siblisresearch.com/data/market-cap-to-gdp-ratios/).

Siegel, Jeremy J. 2016. "The Shiller CAPE Ratio: A New Look." *Financial Analysts Journal*, vol. 72, no. 3 (May/June): 41–50.

Singh, Mohini, and Sandra Peters. 2016. *Data and Technology: Transforming the Financial Information Landscape*. Charlottesville, VA: CFA Institute (June): www.cfapubs.org/doi/pdf/10.2469/ccb.v2016.n7.1.

Slager, Alfred. 2017. "The Trustee Perspective: Active Manager Still Has a Place." *IPE Magazine* (3 February): www.ipe.com/reports/special-reports/active-management/the-trustee-perspective-active-manager-still-has-a-place/10017401.article.

Soe, Aye M., and Ryan Poirier. 2016. "Does Past Performance Matter? The Persistence Scorecard." S&P Dow Jones Research (December): https://us.spindices.com/documents/spiva/persistence-scorecard-december-2016.pdf.

Sorensen, Eric H. 2017. "Investment Insight: Smart Data, Big Beta and the Evolving Land of Quant." PanAgora (May): https://publishing.dealogic.com/Nomura/PanAgora.pdf.

Sorensen, Eric, and David Williamson. 1985. "Some Evidence on the Value of Dividend Discount Models." *Financial Analysts Journal*, vol. 41, no. 6 (November/December): 60–69.

S&P. 2017. "S&P 500 Buybacks Total $135.3 Billion for Q4 2016, Decline for Full-Year 2016." Standard & Poor's (22 March): http://us.spindices.com/documents/index-news-and-announcements/20170322-sp-500-buybacks-q4-2016-pr.pdf.

Straehl, Philip U., and Roger G. Ibbotson. 2015. "The Supply of Stock Returns: Adding Back Buybacks." Morningstar working paper (17 December): http://corporate1.morningstar.com/WorkArea/DownloadAsset.aspx?id=13346.

Tergesen, Anne, and Jason Zweig. 2016. "The Dying Business of Picking Stocks." *Wall Street Journal* (17 October): www.wsj.com/articles/the-dying-business-of-picking-stocks-1476714749.

"Valuing Private Companies." 2016. *Investopedia* (16 November): www.investopedia.com/articles/fundamental-analysis/11/valuing-private-companies.asp#ixzz4c2kLLaTK.

Wang, Lu. 2016a. "There's Only One Buyer Keeping S&P 500's Bull Market Alive." Bloomberg (14 March): www.bloomberg.com/news/articles/2016-03-14/there-s-only-one-buyer-keeping-the-s-p-500-s-bull-market-alive.

———. 2016b. "Bull Market Losing Big Ally as Buybacks Fall Most since 2009." Bloomberg (16 May): www.bloomberg.com/news/articles/2016-05-16/bull-market-losing-biggest-ally-as-buybacks-fall-most-since-2009.

Werner, Richard. 2012. "The Quantity Theory of Credit and Some of Its Applications." Working paper, Robinson College, University of Cambridge.

Wicksell, Knut. 1898. *Geldzins und Güterpreise* (first English ed.: *Interest and Prices*, 1936). London: Macmillan (available as a PDF file or ebook from the Ludwig von Mises Institute, https://mises.org/library/interest-and-prices).

Williams, John Burr. 1938. *The Theory of Investment Value*. Cambridge, MA: Harvard University Press.

World Bank. 2015. "Market Capitalization of Listed Domestic Companies (% of GDP)." World Federation of Exchanges database (http://data.world-bank.org/indicator/CM.MKT.LCAP.GD.ZS?end=2015&locations=US&start=1975&view=chart).

Xiong, James X., Roger G. Ibbotson, Thomas M. Idzorek, and Peng Chen. 2010. "The Equal Importance of Asset Allocation and Active Management." *Financial Analysts Journal*, vol. 66, no. 2 (March/April): 22–30.

Yardeni, Edward. 2017. "Bull by the Tail." *Dr. Ed's Blog* (5 April): http://blog.yardeni.com/2017/04/bull-by-tail.html.

Zörgiebel, Severin Johannes. 2016a. "Valuation of IPOs with Negative Earnings." Working paper, Goethe University Frankfurt (June).

———. 2016b. "The Rise of the Unicorns: How Media Affects Start-Up Valuations." Working paper, Goethe University Frankfurt (July): https://papers.ssrn.com/sol3/papers.cfm?abstract_id=2808458.

Named Endowments

The CFA Institute Research Foundation acknowledges with sincere gratitude the generous contributions of the Named Endowment participants listed below.

Gifts of at least US$100,000 qualify donors for membership in the Named Endowment category, which recognizes in perpetuity the commitment toward unbiased, practitioner-oriented, relevant research that these firms and individuals have expressed through their generous support of the CFA Institute Research Foundation.

Ameritech
Anonymous
Robert D. Arnott
Theodore R. Aronson, CFA
Asahi Mutual Life Insurance Company
Batterymarch Financial
   Management
Boston Company
Boston Partners Asset Management,
   L.P.
Gary P. Brinson, CFA
Brinson Partners, Inc.
Capital Group International, Inc.
Concord Capital Management
Dai-Ichi Life Insurance Company
Daiwa Securities
Mr. and Mrs. Jeffrey Diermeier
Gifford Fong Associates
Investment Counsel Association
   of America, Inc.
Jacobs Levy Equity Management
John A. Gunn, CFA
John B. Neff, CFA
Jon L. Hagler Foundation
Long-Term Credit Bank of Japan, Ltd.
Lynch, Jones & Ryan, LLC
Meiji Mutual Life Insurance
   Company

Miller Anderson & Sherrerd, LLP
Nikko Securities Co., Ltd.
Nippon Life Insurance Company of
   Japan
Nomura Securities Co., Ltd.
Payden & Rygel
Provident National Bank
Frank K. Reilly, CFA
Salomon Brothers
Sassoon Holdings Pte. Ltd.
Scudder Stevens & Clark
Security Analysts Association
   of Japan
Shaw Data Securities, Inc.
Sit Investment Associates, Inc.
Standish, Ayer & Wood, Inc.
State Farm Insurance Company
Sumitomo Life America, Inc.
T. Rowe Price Associates, Inc.
Templeton Investment Counsel Inc.
Frank Trainer, CFA
Travelers Insurance Co.
USF&G Companies
Yamaichi Securities Co., Ltd.

Senior Research Fellows
Financial Services Analyst Association

For more on upcoming Research Foundation
publications and webcasts, please visit
www.cfainstitute.org/learning/foundation.

Research Foundation monographs
are online at www.cfapubs.org.

RESEARCH FOUNDATION
CONTRIBUTION FORM

☑ **Yes**, I want the Research Foundation to continue to fund innovative research that advances the investment management profession. Please accept my tax-deductible contribution at the following level:

Thought Leadership Circle..................... US$1,000,000 or more
Named Endowment .... US$100,000 to US$999,999
Research Fellow .... US$10,000 to US$99,999
Contributing Donor............................US$1,000 to US$9,999
Friend .... Up to US$999

I would like to donate US$ _____.

☐ My check is enclosed (payable to the CFA Institute Research Foundation).
☐ I would like to donate appreciated securities (send me information).
☐ Please charge my donation to my credit card.
      ☐ VISA   ☐ MC   ☐ Amex   ☐ Diners

| | | | | | | | | | | | | | | | | | | | |

Card Number

_____ / _____   _____
Expiration Date   Name on card   P L E A S E   P R I N T
☐ Corporate Card
☐ Personal Card   _____
                                          Signature

☐ This is a pledge. Please bill me for my donation of US$_____
☐ I would like recognition of my donation to be:
      ☐ Individual donation   ☐ Corporate donation   ☐ Different individual

_____
      PLEASE PRINT NAME OR COMPANY NAME AS YOU WOULD LIKE IT TO APPEAR

PLEASE PRINT   ☐ Mr.☐ Mrs.☐ Ms.   MEMBER NUMBER_____

_____
Last Name (Family Name)   First (Given Name)   Middle Initial

_____
Title

_____
Address

_____
City   State/Province   Country ZIP/Postal Code

Please mail this completed form with your contribution to:
The CFA Institute Research Foundation • P.O. Box 2082
Charlottesville, VA 22902-2082 USA

For more on the CFA Institute Research Foundation, please visit www.cfainstitute.org/learning/foundation/Pages/index.aspx.